The Epic of

E Keble Chatterton

Table of Contents

PREFACE

THE following pages are concerned with one of the most wonderful episodes in our history. My aim has been, firstly, to indicate the activities which made this evacuation necessary; but, secondly, to show what happened to the various types of craft. Truth is not one-sided, so that occasionally some overlapping and repetition may be inevitable.

For instance, the same incident may look quite different when viewed respectively from a destroyer, a packet-boat, and a tug. Intentionally my desire has been to present this thrilling story from many angles.

I have been able from personal conversations with, and the reports written by, commanding officers themselves specially concerned, to offer these first-hand narratives so closely following actual events that their authenticity cannot be called into question and time is unable to deteriorate.

Generally this Dunkirk episode was the Merchant Navy's greatest contribution towards national aid, and for that reason particular stress has been laid thereon. I am grateful to shipowners, the Port of London Authority, the Ministry of Information, the Ministry of Shipping, the Admiralty, and many others who have so courteously assisted me.

E. KEBLE CHATTERTON.

CHAPTER I — HOW IT ALL BEGAN

IT was in the early hours of May 10, 1940, that the greatest and swiftest drama of modem European civilisation began to be enacted when at 3-30 a.m. German aircraft suddenly started bombing barracks at The Hague. Only two hours earlier some eight hundred Dutch troops had been out on night exercises. Thus, whilst asleep on their beds, most of these tired men were blown into the next world.

Simultaneously the Nazis destroyed Holland's aerodromes, then transport planes in considerable numbers flew over escorted by Messerschmitts and dropped soldiers around The Hague by means of parachutes, whilst squadrons of Heinkels rained leaflets summoning the population to surrender. "Opposition is useless. You are already surrounded," said the ruthless invaders.

On the very eve of invading the Low Countries, Germany had solemnly pledged her intention to respect Holland's neutrality and freedom. Such an assurance was as typically German as her callousness and brutality. With a perfectly organised war machine geared for high speed, an amazing momentum of mechanised onslaughts, and a diabolical co-operation with spies and traitors, the enemy had little difficulty in imposing his will.

Surprise hammered its blows everywhere, although the Dutch for three days knew that attack was imminent: but how many of those stolid, easy-going people had ever imagined that so much treachery could be in their midst? That those who for years had posed as friends and accepted Dutch hospitality, now might turn on their former hosts with firearms and kill decent citizens?

Not merely Holland, but Luxemburg and Belgium were over-run. These three countries appealed to Britain and France for aid, which promptly was forthcoming. Yet the pace of events, the rate of big developments, paralysed the imagination. Already on this same day a Dutch seaplane carrying two members of Queen Wilhelmina's Government with difficulty escaped German attention, fled across the North Sea and arrived among the bathers on Brighton beach. Two days later the Nazis were holding several vital parts of Rotterdam, where fierce conflagrations raged skywards; many more parachutist invaders alighted around The Hague, as previously planned, with persistent continuity; whilst simultaneously German mobile units from Aix la Chapelle were racing over the Belgian frontier to cross in the Maastricht area that Albert Canal whose official opening had preceded the war by less than a month.

It will always seem incredible to any honest mind that on Thursday, May 9 — the day immediately preceding invasion of these countries — an article was published in the "Muenchener Neueste Nachrichten" denying any intention on the part of Germany to attack the Netherlands or Belgium. The article said:

"It is one of the most impertinent lies issued by the British Ministry of Information, mostly through neutral channels, that a German attack is planned on Belgium and Holland. This British lie is too cheap for anybody either in Germany or any other country to believe."

But it was the enemy who lied, and fabricated excuses without shame. A German memorandum handed to the Dutch and Belgian Governments accused Britain and France of planning an imminent invasion of the three countries with the latter's knowledge, as preliminary to attacking the Ruhr. This suggestion Jkhr. van Kleffens, Dutch Foreign Minister, rejected "with indignation", whilst M. Spaak, Belgium's Foreign Minister, in deprecating vigorously against Germany's "crime" reminded the Nazis that "no ultimatum, no Note, no protest was presented to the Belgian Government, which learned only by the assault itself that the pacts between Belgium and Germany had been broken."

A daring attempt by the Nazi Air Force to capture Queen Wilhelmina only just failed. A flight of Junkers, each carrying a score of soldiers, landed on the Valkenburg Airport near the Queen's summer villa at Ruygenhoek, whilst other kidnappers alighted at Delft, several miles south of The Hague. Luckily the scheme to cut off The Hague from the rest of Holland, whilst Queen and Government were being carried into captivity, failed to ripen. Her Majesty escaped by warship to England, the Grand Duchess Charlotte from Luxemburg got away barely in time to northern France, but whilst bombs were coming with the dawn on to the Schiphol aerodrome at Amsterdam others were being showered upon Antwerp and every Belgian aerodrome.

And King Leopold?

Surely he was sincere when early on that Saturday morning his message to the nation was broadcast by the Belgian radio. "We had faithfully discharged our duty of neutrality," he said. "France and Great Britain have given us their support, and their first troops are already on their way to meet ours. The struggle will be hard, but no one can doubt its ultimate outcome."

Certainly no one expected that, a fortnight later, this same Leopold would decide to capitulate and basely desert the Allies whose assistance he so earnestly pleaded. That request was made on May 10. Next day the Guards Brigade left Lille, where they had spent winter and spring. At last a war of movement after hibernating! So whilst Admiral of the Fleet Sir Roger Keyes was on his way as additional Naval Attaché to afford special liaison with the Belgian King, British troops were advancing towards the east of Brussels and Louvain, where heavy fighting immediately took place.

Thus had been inaugurated the terrific tragic drama which must end almost as suddenly as it began. Yet not before weeks of pain should utterly transform the map of Europe. From the first this triple invasion was condemned by the Pope, whose messages of sympathy to King Leopold, Queen Wilhelmina, and the Grand Duchess respectively stressed "the re-establishment of full liberty and the independence", "the re-establishment of justice and liberty", "liberty and independence".

Liberty, Justice, Independence: these were exactly the reasons which inspired our men as they now clashed into conflict against the German mechanised hordes. By Monday May 13 a violent and extensive battle of tanks was raging in northeast Belgium — indeed along the entire front from Holland through Belgian territory towards the French frontier; but the centre of this gigantic operation focused itself in the direction of the line formed by the defence River Meuse-Longwy-Montmedy through the forest-clad slopes of the Ardennes. This densely wooded area of oaks and beeches, of barren moors and fertile river valleys, became the background for a series of wedge-driving tactics that were to show themselves as the Germans essential purpose. One wedge driven between Dutch and Belgians, another wedge between the French line, and subsequently yet a third thrust into the Anglo-French co-operation.

The onslaught developed with startling rapidity and massed attacks, with a directness of purpose against key-positions. Whilst the forts of Liege were being subjected to elephantine blows, the lengthy Moerdyk Bridge was captured by treachery and domination. As you come up the turgid channel of Hollandsch Diep this railway span stands prominently against the sky, and Moerdyk Harbour slightly to the westward but on the Diep's southern side is normally used by Dutch motor and sailing vessels which trade along the inland waters. Nor did the Germans neglect to secrete in this lonely spot a suitable craft wherein troops lay hidden and ready to leap forth at the chosen moment. Almost before the Hollanders could realise what had happened, Moerdyk Bridge was seized, and with it passed the link which connected northern to southern Holland, besides finally severing all connection with Belgium.

This wedge created the greatest discouragement on May 14. The area between Moerdyk and The Hague being now generally under German control, northeast Holland having also been occupied by the enemy right down to the Zuyder Zee's shores, and Rotterdam having fallen, the Commander-in-Chief of the Netherlands Army at 11 p.m. that night ordered his troops to cease fire "in order to save the civilian population and to avoid further bloodshed". Only in the southwestern province of Zeeland, which included Middleburg, Flushing, and several small islands, did resistance for a while continue.

Thus within five short days Holland passed under the Nazi yoke. Nor was that all.

The great battle raging through northeast Belgium along a front of 200 miles developed on May 15 a vigour comparable with that of some devastating hurricane. Our Brigade of Guards was engaged in heavy fighting to the east of Brussels and Louvain. Hordes of German bombers operated over the scene dive-attacking British troops and destroying roads behind, whilst long treks of refugees, struggling afoot or on bicycles, blocked roadways, and bursting shells increased the chaos.

Louvain, whose famous library had suffered destruction in 1914 and had afterwards been rebuilt, was again at the mercy of Germans, houses and railway station too were bombed. British forces were compelled to withdraw, on the night of May 16-17 Louvain once more fell into the enemy's hands, and our troops retreated to the westward of Brussels. For a while they halted beyond the River Dendre at Okegem, only to resume their withdrawal on May 21 to the line of the Scheldt near Roubaix.

Little protection did this river afford them, inasmuch as the French and Belgians having opened dykes to flood the country at other points caused the normal 9-feet depth to be changed into only 1½ feet. It was thus that further withdrawal became necessary to Tourcoing next day, and that after this short excursion into Belgium the Guards were almost back again in that area north of Lille whence they had set out a fortnight previously.

The situation had indeed taken a most serious complexion, and in a later chapter we shall perceive how this was appreciated both by the Admiralty and Ministry of Shipping. Let us keep in mind, particularly, two dates, the 14th and 19th of May, for future study. Louvain, Malines, Brussels under German domination, violent tank and plane attacks never easing up: that was the picture beneath a clear blue sky. And the enemy's strategy now had shown itself plainer still.

For whilst Dutch refugees of all sorts — fishermen, members of their parliament, journalists, mothers and children — were crossing the North Sea in trawlers and yachts to England (though some, after evading bombs, blundered to their deaths among mines), France was contending, so to speak, with her back against the wall. By Tuesday, May 14, the Germans utterly regardless of human lives were flinging themselves and their tanks against the Sedan salient in the firm determination to break through the French line no matter what the cost.

The Zeeland Islands, after stubborn fighting by combined Allied forces, were evacuated, the harbour facilities of Flushing — Holland's southernmost gateway both of its vast canal system and its railways — had been destroyed, petrol tanks set alight, and the dockyard where so many Dutch warships used to be launched now rendered ineffective. But, with Nazi activities concentrated overwhelmingly against France in the Sedan area, a fresh tornado of tank tactics burst forth from their Ardennes concealment.

Properly to show all that was happening at this time we should need something more than the printed word arranged in consecutive paragraphs. The modern cinema, with its impressionistic pictures, its flashbacks and intercepting glimpses, alone could provide simultaneous narrative. Whilst one furious drama was ending in Holland, another had still to gain its climax in France.

As to the former we can keep alive in imagination the laying of German magnetic mines outside the Dutch ports, the escape of Netherlandish naval and mercantile ships, the counter-mining by British units, the despatch across the North Sea to Ymuiden of a flotilla of our Motor Torpedo Boats. Now Ymuiden is just over a hundred miles distant from Lowestoft, which in reckoning of time meant only a very few hours. Great possibilities suggested themselves.

After you enter the Outer Harbour between two moles, you come to three pairs of locks which give access to the North Sea Canal, that brings liners and all sorts of shipping at the end of thirteen miles to the port of Amsterdam. From this city, in turn, exit from the North Sea Canal is obtained through the Orange Locks on to the Zuyder Zee for any craft drawing not more than 5 feet of water.

Behold, then, this flotilla racing down the smooth waterway in the hope of demonstrating naval power on the almost enclosed Zuyder Zee. This might have led to an exceptionally interesting naval engagement: a wonderfully unique battle — had it encountered the Nazi Motor Torpedo Boats just then on their way from Germany. But a trap was evolving itself, and the door about to be shut.

It was obvious that Amsterdam would presently collapse; already the oil tanks were blazing, and withdrawal down the canal must therefore be made immediately. But not long after Ymuiden's sluices had once more been negotiated, a British naval lieutenant succeeded pluckily in sealing these up by the simple effective method of employing blockships: for you can create a wonderful amount of obstruction with a little luck, one trawler, one ore-laden steamer, and smart seamanship. A 12,000-tons liner equally sufficed to cork up the third lock. Thus as a port for deep-draught vessels Amsterdam was rendered impossible.

And so we could continue to present pictures of British destroyers dodging bombers in that narrow waterway leading past the Hook of Holland towards Rotterdam; gallant Marines as always doing their work unostentatiously despite dangers; refugees being snatched from beneath Nazi eyes; thrilling voyages over the sea back to England.

But our subject is the Evacuation of Dunkirk, and our immediate concern is to indicate in what manner that greatest of all withdrawals became necessary as well as practicable. Nor can we delay our story to relate how by "a particularly desperate and gallant exploit" (as the British Admiralty phrased it) two of Holland's submarines, "O-23" and "O-24", which had just been built at Rotterdam for the East Indies, got away barely in time, evaded magnetic mines and dodged the capture which Nazis had intended.

It will suffice if we indicate quite briefly how the Dutch destroyer "Van Gaelen" maintained by her plucky enterprise the sea's best traditions. Let it be stressed that the Netherlands, though small in European territory, are the world's third greatest colonial power, for which reason her East Indian contingent has always formed the strongest part of this Royal Dutch Navy.

Both the cruisers "Tromp" (3400 tons armed with six 5.9-inch and eight anti-aircraft guns) and "De Ruyter" (6100 tons, armed with seven 5.9-inch and ten anti-aircraft guns) were recognised as excellent, modem vessels able to do their 32 knots. Some of the Dutch Naval units certainly were presently represented in the historic evacuation of Dunkirk, and one was lost, whilst others went down fighting at the time of the German invasion.

This "Van Gaelen" lived through a hectic interlude before finally paying the penalty. It was she who acted so efficiently when German troop-carrying 'planes landed on the beach at Scheveningen, these sands having been specially chosen by the enemy because of their contiguity to The Hague with its royal palace and government offices. From the sea "Van Gaelen" (1300 tons, 36 knots) with her four 4.7-inch guns crumpled up these aircraft and afterwards steamed round the corner up the mine-infested Maas towards Rotterdam with the object of shelling the Germans out of the adjacent Waalhaven aerodrome. The Nazis replied with their dive-bombers, which thirty times swooped down on this vessel but did not prevent "Van Gaelen" from maintaining a steady fire. Only at the thirty-first effort did these hostile aircraft succeed in registering a direct hit, which put the destroyer into a sinking condition though she was beached and her crew proceeded to continue fighting on land.

It will always be a matter for congratulation that the greater part of the Dutch Navy, though battle scarred, managed after the four days' intensive contending to reach England and that others, which had not been quite completed at the shipyards when trouble developed, were towed safely across to a British port. The nett result was that whilst some could be handed over to our dockyards for subsequent completion and fitting out as part of our naval forces, the rest required only minor attention before taking up active duties.

The two cruisers were responsible for carrying Princess Juliana with her two children to Canada and assisted in convoying Canadian troops over to England. Considering the matter as a whole, the Nazis by their invasion of Holland did us quite a good turn: not merely were Dutch gunboats and destroyers entrusted with such duties as local defence of harbours and estuaries, minesweeping, minelaying, hunting U-boats, but the Dutch Fleet Air Arm was able to swell our sky squadrons.

Another most valuable addition was the aid which Holland could bring with her Merchant Navy. Three million tons had made her shipping second only to that of France, and after allowing for war losses during the pre-invasion period there still remained 180 ocean-going vessels and 250 trading coasters — or roughly a million tons — which our Ministry of Shipping chartered alike for carrying British exports abroad and bringing us raw materials and food. This was particularly to be appreciated when convoys were singled out for attack by U-boats, bombs, and shells.

Thus, though Hitler might with his land forces conquer cities and territory, he could not interfere either with the Dutch Mercantile Marine voyaging along the trade routes or sweep down against its normal activities in the Pacific and Indian Oceans. For such ambitions he would need superiority of sea-power, which was denied him.

CHAPTER II — TOWARDS DUNKIRK

THE Maginot Line, on which so many millions of francs had been expended and so much reliance placed for impregnability, extended from Basle on the Swiss frontier up to Longwy on the frontier of Luxemburg, whence a line of lighter fortifications continued to the North Sea.

Now after Holland, Belgium, and Luxemburg had been invaded, the left wing of the French Army advanced from these fortifications between Sedan and the sea, and pivoted on Sedan entered Belgium. Whether it was part of Leopold's treachery to entrap these forces, to deliver them as easy victims for the Germans, need not now be discussed. But the point was later stressed by Monsieur Reynaud, whilst still French Premier and Defence Minister, that when the Germans launched their unexpected onslaught, they found the crest of France's Army established behind the Meuse between Namur and Sedan in no perfect strength. Why so weak hereabouts?

The answer is that because the Meuse had been considered redoubtable and impossible to be crossed by the enemy, only the weakest French divisions — those less well trained and with inferior officers — were considered adequate. Surely the Germans would never try to smash their way through the difficult Ardennes?

Actually General Gamelin's troops in this sector were too few in numbers, and too widely spread apart, his best soldiery being on the French wing marching into Belgium. But if the Meuse was a rivet difficult to defend, the infiltration for the enemy turned out to be comparatively easy. And on the top of this unfortunate truth must be added those incredible mistakes which comprised neglect to destroy vital bridges.

That was why German armoured divisions, preceded by fighter aeroplanes, had little trouble in getting across, scattering the indifferently trained and badly led troops, throwing General Corap's Army into confusion, and permitting a fatal breach to be made where resistance should have been unbroken. Thus, by the employment of surprise, Nazi massive motorised divisions co-operating with aircraft in new methods, the creation of disorder in the French rear by parachute raids (which in Belgium had enabled the strongest of Liege's forts to be seized), the subtle circulation of false news, and unauthorised orders given by telephone for creating hurried evacuations, a colossal disaster was set going from which France could never recover. May 14, then, is one of the great dates in history: the peak of France's modern progress, the beginning of her quick descent.

Pitiable it is to watch this collapse gaining impetus daily down the slippery path that could lead in but one direction. Infuriating to realise that, as in Holland, so in France, the shameless help by secret agents and traitors, either previously posted by the enemy at important centres or infiltrated across the border among Belgian refugees, should have been able to throw the work of civil authorities into confusion.

Gamelin was dismissed summarily, to be succeeded by the 73-years-old Weygand of whom much was expected though little more than disappointment evolved. Although in England there had been born a new confidence when change of Premiers enabled Mr Churchill to succeed Mr Chamberlain, a similar succession in France permitting the octogenarian Marshal Petain to receive Monsieur Reynaud's office could in no wise improve upon the danger which threatened.

Nothing could make up for that deadly breach, no amount of clever strategy or earnest exhortation could succeed in closing the ever-widening gap which now extended between Arras on the north and Amiens on the south. It was as if doors had been flung wide to admit an almighty torrent which no force could stem. By May 23 the Germans had verily driven their latest and most powerful wedge with depth and power, so that the Allies' position now was as follows:

In the north a powerful army of British, French, and Belgian troops were holding a solid, continuous, well organised front that extended from the sea opposite Flushing via the Scheldt and Valenciennes to Arras. In the south, stretching from the English Channel, was a line of French positions roughly along the Somme, Aisne, Rethel, Montmedy, connecting with the Maginot Line in the direction of the Swiss frontier.

The immediate German aim was so to surround the Northern Army that it could be annihilated; for which reason German planes on May 22 had already begun to bomb Dunkirk — the port through which British troops were receiving stores and munitions — and on May 23 the Nazis made contact with the Allied forces holding the suburbs of Boulogne. Next day our defending force had to be withdrawn from that port. Similarly, by rapid mechanical advance round the Allies' rear, light German units pushed their way to the outskirts of Calais.[1] In short, the enemy, by aiming to cut off the Channel ports, congratulated himself that nothing could prevent this Northern Allied Army from complete and entire destruction: British, French, and Belgian soldiers would be mopped up into death or captivity.

It was on May 27 that the British Army was ordered to retreat from Tourcoing, but owing to the roads being blocked by French troops and refugees it was not till May 29 that most of the British Army reached the neighbourhood of Furnes, where the Guards held the canal south of the town against German forces pressing forward to prevent the B.E.F.'s escape towards Dunkirk. Heavy fighting and losses were inevitable; after an anxious time our men abandoned Furnes, and early on June 1 withdrew to La Panne.

During seventy-two hours at Furnes the Guards under Brigadier J. A. C. Whitaker had held this key position, repulsing vastly superior forces, and thus enabled thousands of British troops to pass through Dunkirk and board the ships, and so to England. It should, however, be mentioned that originally too much hope had been placed on La Panne, and we shall note in subsequent pages that such units as barges and motorboats were sent hither in a move which became impossible.

After reaching La Panne in the darkness and finding no shipping visible till early dawn revealed the latter a mile from the beach, there was some morseing with a pocket torch, and boats went off to the soldiers despite heavy bombing. But the rest of the men marched along the shores to Dunkirk, and later this morning of June 1 were embarking thence.

The enemy from May 27 was already claiming that "The Great Battle of Flanders" had reached its zenith, that the Allies were hemmed in, that north of Valenciennes they had made a wide gap through the French frontier fortifications, and that west of Valenciennes they had crossed the Scheldt Canal, captured Douai and — most significantly — the German Air Force had begun bombing the communication line running to Zeebrugge, Ostend, and Dunkirk. *On paper*, then, the Anglo-French were hemmed in and nothing could rescue them from utter perdition. Then, to top the lot, followed the Belgian capitulation.

It is unfortunately true that for some time the British and French had been vaguely suspicious of Leopold, but were in the closest touch with him till 8 p.m. of Monday, May 27. That night, Germans were allowed to pass through Belgian lines without resistance and attack Allies in the rear. The result was that next day the B.E.F. and French found themselves being assaulted in the rear as well as on the left flank, and matters were so grave that on May 29 Mr Churchill, Prime Minister, did not hesitate to inform the House of Commons that the Belgian "surrender adds appreciably to the grievous peril of the British and French Armies." Whilst promising a further statement "early next week," he added, "Meanwhile the House should prepare itself for hard and heavy tidings". That night the public was further warned by Mr Duff Cooper, Minister of Information, who in broadcasting on the radio foreshadowed that "it will be necessary to withdraw our Army from the position they now occupy."

Actually that withdrawal was already begun, but the remarkable feature is that after marching and fighting continuously ever since about May 14, the B.E.F., though bereft of almost any rest, never forfeited their discipline or morale. It mattered not that they were shelled and attacked by tanks throughout a fortnight, that communications were perpetually bombed from the air, that roads were blocked by the thousands of refugees, our troops — splendidly led by their officers — were in fine fettle, though weary.

This is not the place to stay and inquire into King Leopold's treacherous act. It is enough to state that at his Château Wyondal, near Thourout, some twelve miles southwest of Bruges a stormy session was held that weekend, when on Saturday May 25 he informed the four members of his Cabinet that he desired to capitulate. The four Ministers rejected the suggestion, and walked out. Admiral Sir Roger Keyes left the Belgian Court, and was back in London by Monday night, May 27.

The world seemed to have gone mad in a summer which was beginning with warmth and sunshine that had rarely been surpassed. Whilst children played in the sea along the English resorts, gunfire rumbled so loudly from the French coasts that the people of Kent had little sleep for several nights, doors burst open, pictures fell down and a couple of schoolboys were hurt when a classroom wall collapsed, and one child had his leg broken. It was ominous, too, that the War Office on May 26 warned anxious relatives that soldiers just now could not communicate with the same regularity as in the past.

Something tremendous was happening, many were the hints, but the newspapers with wise restraint did not excite the nation's eagerness. By special request of our King a day of National Prayer was decided upon for Sunday, May 26, and millions flocked within churches to petition for deliverance from as great a crisis as had ever threatened our existence. Tonight Monsieur Reynaud visited London to confer with our Prime Minister. What was in the wind?

It had been known in diplomatic quarters for some while that Leopold had been showing a non-co-operative attitude towards the Allies, yet he had asked for our help and we had gone to his aid. It was a grievous shock that 300,000 Belgians should surrender and lay down their arms at the most unfortunate moment. We could understand something of his excitable, neurotic, emotional and uncertain behaviour, but could scarcely pardon it.

Meanwhile the gap, which the Germans had burst through, was still unclosed. The enemy were pressing forward their mechanised units and motorised infantry through the bottle-neck between Bapaume and Amiens, some going towards Boulogne and Calais, whilst British and French were defending the essential supply port of Dunkirk in the south and west. As we shall see presently, the enemy entered Calais via Sangatte from Boulogne: he was able also to occupy Ostend from May 29 and to operate his motorboats off Nieuport. But this night, whilst Allied troops were fighting a terrific rearguard action towards the coast, the lock-gates on May 29 were opened to let the tide flood the low-lying plains southwest of Dunkirk and around Nieuport — an action to which Leopold had been opposed. Under the gallant Vice-Admiral Abrial the French at Dunkirk were well entrenched resisting the oncoming Germans, and thereby made it possible for the embarkation of those others. For this self-sacrificing duty we are bound to concede the utmost thanks.

Such, then, were the events which led to the necessity for the great withdrawal from Dunkirk. There is a terrible grandeur in the undertaking, which does not lessen as we contemplate this from afar. The most breathless fortnight in our history, with its majestic drama and high gamble for human lives, was to turn a rout into — certainly not a victory over arms but — a triumph over obstacles which seemed totally impracticable. It was only by a super-effort of the British nation that, officially and individually, the impossible was attained.

Let us, then, first see what steps were taken by the government departments and how the ships plus the men contrived to extract from the tightest of corners an Army menaced with surrender or destruction.

CHAPTER III — CALAIS AND BOULOGNE

SOMETHING had to be done. If these vital harbours could not be defended, then they must be rendered useless.

The British Navy acted with amazing vigour. At 6-30 a.m. on the tenth there arrived in Dover scores of naval officers, seamen, Royal Engineers. Why had they come? Not one of them knew till Vice-Admiral Bertram H. Ramsay sent them across the sea for demolition duties, which eventually included Flushing, Rotterdam, Antwerp, and other ports. Presently, too, followed detachments of Marines, Guards, and others.

Still the Nazis with remarkable speed raced coastward, British forces were hurried over the Channel to hold Calais and Boulogne, and there performed such deeds of gallantry, such incredible displays of heroism against superior strength that we must first perceive these pictures before reaching the sand dunes of Dunkirk. For a new and more wonderful story was to be written on stones already greyed by time's events.

Nearly six centuries ago Calais was captured by the bravery of English soldiers. In May 1940 it was defended by English warriors, who bled and died with a self-sacrifice that would have been the admiration of their mediaeval ancestors. If bows and arrows had been replaced by Bren guns and bayonets, the spirit of our fathers in nowise was altered. Let it be appreciated that on this Calais effort depended the possibility of Dunkirk's evacuation: any withdrawal of the beleaguered British Expeditionary Force a few miles further up the coast pivoted on what could be accomplished in that gateway to France through which unthinking tourists used to make for Paris.

So with orders to "Hold out till the end", Brigadier Claude Nicholson — one of the most brilliant officers who ever passed through the Staff College, whose brains and driving powers matched his foresight and personal bravery — was despatched from England with 3000 troops composed of the King's Royal Rifle Corps, Rifle Brigade, Royal Tank Regiment and the Queen Victoria's Rifles (a London Territorial battalion). This was on Tuesday, May 21, and bad luck dogged them from the beginning.

Owing to the lack of stevedores and other difficulties the Rifle Brigade were unable to land three-quarters of their vehicles, equipment and ammunition. East and west of the town, guarding the roads from Dunkirk and Boulogne, companies were sent forth but casualties quickly mounted, German tanks and mechanised infantry gradually drove the British troops and a thousand French units back and back inside the city.

By Wednesday, May 22, the Nazis had been raiding and injuring Calais to some purpose, doing such special work as damaging the lock-gates which give access to the inner basin. It chanced that Captain J. Fryer had been sent with the tug "Foremost 87" on a difficult job. She was to go right in and tow out through the gates the S.S. "Katowice" full of refugees into the Calais Roads. This she accomplished, and was next ordered to assist the S.S. "City of Christchurch" from the roadstead to the harbour. This likewise was done, although it rained bombs from the air and three magnetic mines were exploded by the French trawlers sweeping ahead.

Then on the Thursday a curious thing happened. Captain Fryer was ordered to tow the "City of Christchurch" out seawards, but whilst in the act of getting hold of her there came orders to let her alone. Evidently "Fifth Columnists" had been busy, and two men were promptly arrested. However, the tug did not let go the ropes, but later brought her out as originally ordered, and when by Friday that port had become too "hot" the tug was put on other duties. We shall mention her again presently.

On the Thursday, together with "Benlawers" (to be considered on a following page) the S.S. "Kohistan", owned by Messrs Frank Strick, left Dover for Calais. Although the town was being bombed, she finished discharging her cargo by 4 a.m., May 24, as shells came uncomfortably near. When about 8 a.m. she saw the "Benlawers" leave, fires in the town were breaking out with sickly but irresistible virulence, and three hours later the many troops (including 25 wounded) were at last put aboard the "Kohistan".

A pretty warm time she had clearing the breakwater amid the deluge of bursting shells, yet she managed to land her precious burden at Dover through the skill of her Master, Captain Robertson. Of those fatal moments he writes words which no one can possibly read without a sob in the throat. They are the tribute of one brave fellow to others:

"When leaving Calais, men of the Rifle Brigade were lined up alongside the station and waved and cheered us, although they knew they were left to certain death. Their courage and bravery were magnificent … I can only say that, while Britain has men like these and of the Rifle Brigade, we shall never know defeat."

Although unquestionably Brigadier Nicholson's Brigade by holding the enemy's superior forces during four critical days helped to save the B.E.F., yet from the first the loss of our equipment at Calais was a most serious handicap.

When the 60th Rifles and Rifle Brigade disembarked, they moved to a position of assembly by the sands on the Dunkirk side of Calais, waiting for their vehicles and equipment. The first steamer began unloading, but the French stevedores declined to work the crane, and the Royal Engineers, though toiling hard, did not finish their job till early next day.

The vehicle ship with the Rifle Brigade equipment was unloading her cargo, when wounded began reaching the quayside, and the steamer, after taking these aboard, returned to England with motor transport still in the hold. But who gave the orders for this dismissal is still a mystery. Was this one more instance of the Nazis' highly organised spies or traitors at work?

But another transport was destined to play a most exciting and valuable part.

The S.S. "Benlawers" on Thursday, May 23, left Dover laden with motor vehicles for Boulogne escorted by a destroyer. On approaching the French coast such fierce gunfire broke forth that the British destroyer instructed her to 'bout ship and follow astern. Thus they arrived off the narrow entrance to Calais Harbour, across whose mouth, past the two pierheads, the tide rushes so strongly that at Springs it reaches 3 and sometimes 4 knots. Today, however, other features increased a mariner's anxiety.

"Take your ship inside," the destroyer captain ordered, "but I'm afraid you'll have a hot reception."

As the "Benlawers" was steering to pass between the piers with due allowance for the tide, a signal from the shore reached her at the most inconvenient moment. Says her Master, "We picked up a message 'Keep Out', which was flashed from the harbour, but this was easier said than done, owing to the strong tide and the space available for ships of the 'Benlawers'' size."

Finally, after some delay, she did enter and moor alongside the quay with her head pointing towards the mouth ready for any emergency. "It was apparent," realised her Master, "that Calais was not to be held long."

But her much needed cargo? That had to be landed as quickly as possible, because the Nazis were so close at hand. "We can hold the enemy if only we can get the stuff to do it with," Major Attway, from the quay, was saying, and since there were no French stevedores, and the Royal Engineers after toiling three days without a break had become pretty well played out, "Benlawers'" own crew began tackling the job.

They did their best, though considerably hampered first by recurring bomb attacks and later by shell-fire of German howitzers which had been towed into Calais by advance numbers of tanks. By 10 p.m. part of the cargo had been discharged, when things looked so bad that "Benlawers" made all preparations for a hasty departure. Wounded were being brought aboard in dozens, after arriving from inland by train, but it was only on being threatened with the point of a revolver that the French locomotive driver could be forced to keep his train moving.

The situation was becoming worse rapidly, so many bombs and shells falling around this steamer as to render her quayside berth extremely perilous. Meanwhile Army officers came along pleading for more ammunition, so "Benlawers'" crew redoubled their efforts throughout that night and early morning.

About 2 a.m. it was very obvious that any further tarrying would mean her total destruction, for an extra heavy 'whump' against the ship's side indicated that howitzers were making her a fine target. Theoretically "Benlawers" should have been blown to bits; there occurred no explosion though a hole showed itself on the port side and a 5.9-inch shell was found on one of the lorries in the 'tweendeck.

Time enough to depart, if these wounded soldiers were ever to reach England. So they were hurried on board — 700 of them, mostly stretcher cases — with about 50 others comprising troops, prisoners, civilians. In order to afford the best protection for the wounded, accommodation was effected below deck, all the crew yielding up their own berths and cabins. But since the holds were still not emptied of cargo, the remaining guests were compelled to lie on the open deck.

The drama quickened, tension increased, but still permission to proceed did not come. Anxious moments ticked by, the lives of ship and men were suspended uncertainly. Which would come first? Leave to get under way? Or the next shell?

… At last!

"Stand by, for'ard! Leggo, aft!"

Engines began to move, out through the harbour entrance into the tideway the "Benlawers" was quickening her speed, and just as she cleared the piers a heavy fire from shore batteries was directed towards her. Things looked ugly. The enemy, with charts in front of him, well knew that "Benlawers" in clearing the banks which lie seaward of Calais entrance must steam parallel with the coast and so present her broadside as the easiest target.

Then why not go straight on?

Well, there would be too little water for a ship of her size, and unfortunately it was now low tide. An awkward dilemma, when shells were dropping nearer and nearer! Between the Nazi devils and the shallow sea!

"On sizing up the matter", narrates the gallant Master, "I decided it safer to risk crossing the bank and get our stem on to the line of fire."

It was the climax of his eventful voyage. But would "Benlawers" do it? If she stuck … then the Nazis would have a better target still; fixed and motionless.

She reached the shoal patch, her people could feel her 'smelling' the sand. Anything might happen now. Men scarcely dared to speak their thoughts.

Then the crisis passed, the sea deepened.

"We were relieved to feel our speed increase, and with plenty of water under us. The shells were falling close on either side for the first three miles, after which shrapnel was used, inflicting slight injuries on a few of the wounded men."

But six miles from the pierheads "Benlawers" was out of German range, and by 9 a.m. (May 24) had reached Dover. "Jerry" had been cheated of another victim.

The situation at Calais grew from serious to alarming; by Saturday May 25 the enemy's fierce machine-gun fire and heavy artillery bombardment, combined with the continuous blasting from his aircraft, indicated the terrible domination. Nightfall brought a slight respite, the garrison retired within the ancient Citadel or east of the town near the quays. In the former those olden deep casemates now afforded some protection against aerial bombs: the height of mediaeval ramparts proved insurmountable to modern tanks.

Yet after four days, shortage of sleep, shortage of drinking water and food, shortage of ammunition, had begun to tell. About eight o'clock on Sunday morning the Germans sent in a demand for immediate surrender. The Brigadier replied with a firm negative. One hour later a fresh bombardment commenced on Citadel and docks, with incessant relays of dive-bombers. British positions were reduced to shambles, devouring fires spread through the city, hell was let loose, and before 5 p.m. the French Citadel troops surrendered.

Not so the British, although Brig. Nicholson, whose quarters were in the Citadel, was now captured prisoner. Near the quays eastward the Rifle Brigade found themselves surrounded. At dusk they split up into small numbers, continued to fight from house to house, sought every bit of shelter that broken masonry permitted; but the darkness was illumined by the crackling conflagrations vivid as searchlights, and human targets were all too easy for Nazi snipers. Till the limit of physical strength our men persisted in a losing battle, winning for their regiment a new halo in that weatherworn seaport. And so they died. "This action will count among the most heroic deeds in the annals of the British Army", affirmed the War Office later. It has "added another page to the glories of the light divisions", said the Prime Minister to the House of Commons.

Lieut.-Colonel C. B. A. Hoskyns, who commanded the Rifle Brigade, himself a fine leader of men, devoted to the regiment, in peace time famous alike as polo player and as a great amateur theatrical producer, received severe wounds on the third day of battle. Thanks to the pluck of a naval pinnace which crept into the harbour, he was snatched from falling into Nazi hands and brought back to England only to die.

Still, this Calais episode, by detaining two heavy armoured German divisions, which had been intended to cut off the B.E.F., performed the most valuable work. On this very Sunday the great embarkation at Dunkirk was just commencing. Not one man around Calais had perished in vain.

It was on Sunday night that news of the garrison's critical condition reached a certain aerodrome in the south of England. Water and ammunition, the report stated, were required urgently. But water most of all.

Imagine, then, twenty aeroplanes at dawn of Monday soaring into the sky, each loaded in the bomb racks with two cylindrical-shaped containers, and every container carrying ten gallons for thirsty warriors. The water supply in Calais, within my own experience, never had been good, but enemy action by destroying the mains made such fluid precious beyond diamonds.

Zooming across the English Channel, small parachutes ready for lowering the containers, the aeroplanes on their mission of succour made short work of the distance. As they left the coast, the flying men could see twenty miles away immense clouds of smoke rising from the stricken town, and as they came still nearer their eyes beheld ugly gashes of yellow-red flames. Arrived off the Citadel ten aircraft swooped down through the acrid smoke on the western side, whilst the other ten dived towards the eastern end. To avoid error, they descended even to fifty feet, dropped containers dead on the mark, then turned 180 degrees and flew back homewards.

Was the enemy in Calais expectant?

His anti-aircraft guns at once became active; our leading planes escaped easily, but those which followed had to encounter a stiff attack. One was lost, another dived into the ground, and most of them were hit several times. Altogether a pretty hot time was experienced by everyone.

"As I looked back when flying home", related an R.A.F. officer, "I could watch tracer bullets spraying in every direction."

Certainly when these valiant sky-riders reported that despite all difficulties the forty containers had been delivered where meant, not one soldier had been visible in the Citadel. This seemed scarcely surprising at the moment: doubtless the garrison was using the time-stained fortifications as bomb-proof protection. Little did the R.A.F. realise that a few hours previously this garrison had vanished.

Still unaware of this irony, more British aircraft later in the morning, accompanied by dive-bombers to deal with the Nazis drastically, tore through the 1000-feet deep smoke-cloud, dropping into the Citadel small-arms ammunition and hand-grenades. A mighty squadron of thirty-nine war planes thus filled the arc of heaven for a while. Pity that none of our heroes remained to receive the gifts!

To relate all the thrilling happenings during that ever momentous period between May 21 and 27 would be impossible. Even when the fight was over, excitement did not end. Englishmen, as Germans learned in the last war, are still active enough when taken captive. One officer of the Queen Victoria's Rifles made prisoner on the Sunday lost neither hope nor vigilance. Looking out for an opportunity, he cleverly eluded his captors and got away. Making his journey towards the coast, he arrived north of Cape Gris-Nez, there discovered a boat, shoved off, and started to row across the English Channel. Not so foolish an undertaking, since the strong tides can be made to do most of the work. Some of us have rowed over this defile, others have been known to swim. This officer used his oars to such good effect that he arrived safely one mile off the English shore. Along came a patrol drifter who brought him into harbour.

More ambitious was the effort by an officer of the 60th Rifles, who with a couple of Brigade Staff officers likewise dodged the Germans and made a clean get-away. The future, however, looked none too secure. Any hour they might be surprised by some of the enemy hordes. However, travelling the country by night, hiding in the woods during daylight, the trio on June 8 finally reached the River Authie, near Berck. Still the English Channel's width separated them from their homeland. The B.E.F. had long since been taken away from France.

Now in a canal they came across an old motorboat, not in its best health. Also seven French lonely soldiers joined up. Many patient and united efforts to persuade this motor into life brought about little result. Then at last after splutters and reluctance the engine did start and on June 16 the ten got aboard, put forth to sea, crossed the Channel — no longer dotted with Dunkirk transports — and next night at 8 p.m. this band of adventurers saved their daylight to within eight miles of Folkestone. Once more a British destroyer, on sighting the small boat, was able to help distressed soldiers and bring them to the land.

Yes: if it be true, as the history books taught us, that the word 'Calais' was written on the heart of a certain distinguished personage, this same combination of letters will long remain indelible on the hearts of many an Englishman. Nor will the Germans forget, as one Nazi paper proclaimed, that here the Nazis experienced the stiffest resistance of all the war. "The Englishmen had made every house in Calais a fortress."

That same unquenchable courage was to be demonstrated this last week of May when the enemy's rush towards Boulogne made it imperative for us to evacuate 4600 soldiers, and then blow the harbour into uselessness. Few chapters in naval history could ever number so many breathless incidents. With the exception of what happened at Dunkirk, British destroyers by sheer toil and perilous perseverance have not won such undying fame since the days of Dardanelles or the Battle of Jutland.

When the critical day ripened, a demolition party was organised in England consisting of naval seamen, Royal Marines, and a small detachment of R.E.'s. Hurried away in lorries at two hours' notice, they embarked at a south coast port in a destroyer and rushed in the forenoon to land on Boulogne jetty. Their orders were to hold the railway station, fit their demolition charges, note which bridges and lockgates should be blown up presently.

Outside both British and French destroyers lustily shelled the high land northward over which German tanks and mechanised troops were advancing. Things happened with lightning speed, as before. Soon the enemy's field guns were registering on the railway station, light mechanised vehicles followed by tanks and motorised guns came closer. From overhead bombs and machine-guns loosed down death. Sometimes sixty 'planes at a time were co-operating, until the R.A.F. put them to flight.

And now small parties of Nazis became a trickle in the outskirts till the trickle grew into a torrent down the streets. The destroyer had backed out of the narrow harbour entrance to be followed by others bringing more help. But casualties began to multiply. Naval and Military officers decided that Boulogne could not be held against the enemy whose positions controlled harbour and town alike by their guns.

The climax was reached with a violent assault by field artillery, machine-guns, bombs. Waiting till the last batch of our troops had withdrawn far enough, parties of the demolition crews set to work exploding all bridges and important points, cranes, the power-house for pumping the wet-basin; sinking a floating dock therein, together with a

French trawler, whilst some naval stokers with incredible resource and in record time raised steam aboard a French drifter.

Meanwhile the Germans were only 100 yards off, firing their machine-guns, but snipers from a distance of 50 yards were taking toll of our destroyer captains, and thus perished the flotilla's commanding officer.

Yet, with a coolness and persistency which roused every Guardsman's admiration, two destroyers steamed in alongside the jetty, filled up with troops, went out stern first, to be succeeded by others of the six. Tricky work! Attacked by artillery concealed in a wooded hill just above, deluged by pompoms and machine-guns in the second story windows of an hotel 800 yards away, further harassed by lumbering tanks that descended the hill to the foreshore, undismayed either by this tornado of fire or the rising casualties, soldiers and sailors behaved as steadily as if being reviewed by the King.

At point-blank range the destroyers' 4.7's and 4-inch shelled the hillsides, silenced the hotel as it crumpled into masonry; capsized tanks, sent others to flight. The tide was falling, modem destroyers draw quite a lot of water, smart seamanship and stout nerve were needed to avoid grounding.

But finally about 11 p.m. out of the darkened harbour the last destroyer, listing heavily with far too many passengers, emerged stern first past the jetties into open sea. Every living British soldier had been fetched away.

And not one of these destroyers had been sunk.

CHAPTER IV — THE SHIPS GET BUSY

WHEN the new port of Zeebrugge was approaching completion in 1910, and people hinted that without German money the Belgians could not have afforded to create such a white elephant, few Englishmen took much notice. The name had barely come on to the charts. Even naval officers in our country seemed unaware of its existence till after several years.

But if commercial shipping entered infrequently, this enclosed space of three hundred acres with a costly horseshoe shaped mole 1¼ miles long, and a dredged channel leading past an immense breakwater, was obviously meant some day for Germany's use as a naval base. At the shoreward end of the inner harbour project two short piers. Pass through this narrow neck, and you come to lock-gates which enable moderate sized vessels to go up the canal as far as Bruges.

In the first autumn of the last war Germany, after occupying Belgium, wasted no time in turning Zeebrugge's outer harbour into a base for torpedo boats, and soon she also began to send a flotilla of U-boats through the lock-gates up to Bruges where protection from bombs was afforded by concrete shelters. Everyone knows what a menace this Flanders flotilla became against our shipping during the next years. The suggestion to block up the narrow neck and so render approach to the canal useless did not, however, find favour immediately. Indeed not till within seven months of Armistice was the historic effort made when three obsolete cruisers, H.M.S. "Thetis", "Iphigenia" and "Intrepid", on St. George's Day sank themselves in that approach.

Yet, despite all the effort spent, and the diversion created by the simultaneous arrival alongside the horseshoe breakwater by H.M.S. "Vindictive" and her landing party, this blocking raid did not altogether succeed. The U-boats at high water, and with a little care, could always 'wangle' their way out to sea past the sunken cruisers.

Now when history repeated itself in May 1940, and Germany again invaded Holland, it was clear that the British Navy would once more have to tackle the Zeebrugge problem, yet — benefiting by the lessons of

1918 — this sealing up should be attempted with greater simplicity and without diversion.

The selected date of Saturday, May 25, was the eve of Dunkirk's evacuation only a few miles away. But at Zeebrugge the chief difficulty both now and previously was navigational: steering from seaward exactly to pick up the mole's lighthouse, then making a sharp turn fairly close to this breakwater lest the ship gets into the shallow water on the port hand. Next a careful course must be laid towards the two short piers, which are low-lying and not easily visible at a distance. Nor, within the lock-approach, is there room for complicated manoeuvring.

The expedition, consisting of minesweepers, a destroyer, and two blockships with anti-submarine craft, set out, making first for the Wandelaar Lightship, which lies some ten miles from Zeebrugge, and from which an accurate landfall could be made. But would this lightship still be in position? Doubtless the Nazis had already removed it. So we sent a small vessel ahead to indicate the spot, and she actually found the Wandelaar 'watching' as normally. So much the better.

The small vessel then proceeded and dropped a buoy off the breakwater's end to show where the blockships should make their turn and point the way towards the lock approach. Simple enough to state, but not too easy of accomplishment. And this naval enterprise had to be done under cover of night.

Now the blockships' speed was necessarily slow; a destroyer escort accompanied them, and a small detached force swept ahead. Surprise became essential. The enemy must not be made aware. Neither his motor torpedo boats, nor his submarines, must interfere with the project. High water would be about 3-50 (Summer Time) and sunrise an hour later.

All was going very nicely, the mark at the mole end had been laid exactly, but the sudden arrival overhead of a German Air Force bombing squadron caused no little annoyance. For one and a quarter hours their missiles rained down, though our gunfire replied with such effect as to negative the wildest attacks. The small detached force of minesweepers were now making their way home, but, on hearing the pandemonium, gallantly returned half an hour afterwards and again were sent off.

Inside the wide harbour the two blockships came under heavy fire from shore machine-guns, but navigation was far from easy. True both the mole and the houses on the land could be discerned, but over the harbour itself a very thick haze (which so often rises from the Belgian marshes) obscured the low distant piers. Thus it happened that the leading blockship, "Florentino," got too far on the port hand after rounding the mole, hit the shallows and stopped dead. At once an extremely heavy machine-gun fire broke forth, and try as she did with engines going full speed astern this vessel would not move off. The incoming tide slewed her a bit, yet nothing more could be done. All hope of reaching the intended lockgates was out of the question.

It was therefore decided to make the best of things. Both ships had been filled with concrete — they were now sunk about 2000 yards short of the lockgates, yet for many a month would certainly be some hindrance in the main channel.

The rest of this expedition turned about and went home, hindered and disappointed though not beaten. Early on May 27 with two other blockships, "Borodino" and "Atlantic Guide", they tried again with the same plan. No one expected this effort to be any easier, for the enemy had been made alert, and before reaching the Wandelaar a Dornier on patrol flew over, spotted the force and hurried landwards to report. Out soared more reconnaissance 'planes; a contest ensued, yet once more the guiding mark was laid correctly off the mole.

It began to look as if success was assured this time; there would be no too wide turning. Alas! On reaching this mark about 4-45 a.m., the leading blockship's ("Borodino's") steering gear broke down. Just at the most awkward moment! And meanwhile the rattle-rattle-rattle of machine-guns began their music.

The Navy is not unaccustomed to unpleasant contretemps. On St. George's Day, 1918, the three obsolete cruisers could not be steered into their exactly allotted berths. But this May 27 the accident seemed the roughest luck.

Instantly a small escorting steamer was sent to act as tug and bring "Borodino" on her course. Simultaneously the blockship's engineers with remarkable efficiency toiled at the defects, so that altogether no time had been wasted. She continued her progress, entered between the low piers, and though she struck the ground, soon floated off and got to the destined position near the lockgates.

Then a sudden evolution. It was time for every man to quit and take to the boats, for in a few moments the explosion would follow. They were

33

tense seconds as these sailors waited for the explosion. The delay seemed unending. Although the connection to the electric cell had been pressed, nothing happened. What could have gone wrong *this* time?

The evacuating party returned to the ship, investigated, discovered that the cause of trouble lay in the fact that this electric cable by some confounded chance had got foul of the propeller. With quick, cool, energy they set to work, overhauled the connection, again the button was pressed; and now the ship blew the required hole in her hull to settle down as a firm barrier for many a long month.

It had been exciting work as a squadron of fifteen Heinkels sought to interrupt by bombs and bullets, to which our escort vessels outside replied with emphasis. She had come right up to the lockgates, only to find that the Belgians had previously taken the precautions of sinking a dredger across these gates. All the better! The block-ship now rammed her heartily to make doubly sure, blew herself up, and in descending fell over on to the other's stem. Similarly the "Atlantic Guide" immolated herself by the gates. Thus, in short, the whole affair ended with complete satisfaction, the entrance was rendered null and useless. If the Germans should wish to utilise the Bruges Canal again for U-boats they would be grievously disappointed.

Nothing now remained but for the expedition to withdraw. The ships' companies from both steamers pulled at their oars down the bottleneck as if engaged in a keen regatta, reached the other craft, got aboard safely despite the bombers, and sped away back towards England without a casualty having occurred. When one remembers the appalling loss of life and only limited success of the St. George's Day effort, this second sealing of Zeebrugge must stand out as one of the neatest achievements ever performed. Those of us familiar with Zeebrugge and its complexities can only marvel that such smooth working was rendered practicable.

As the men emerged there stood on the mole some Belgians. They knew what had been done, longed to shout their congratulations to British sailors. Waving their hands in glee, as if simulating the movements of a boxer beating his opponent, they bid the blockaders a final farewell.

But now, with the Dutch and Belgian ports demolished, Boulogne pulverised, and Calais held up, the time came for the great withdrawal from Dunkirk. Compelled to retreat, threatened by the Germans with annihilation, there was nothing for the B.E.F. to choose but the sea after the Belgian Army had basely laid down their weapons on May 28. Only by fighting a rearguard action, and the creation of a corridor by local flooding north and south of Dunkirk, could any hope be held out for getting away. It was actually on Sunday, May 26, this evacuation began on a limited scale. Then things happened quickly, immense possibilities widened. Instead of perhaps a lucky 25,000 or so, ten or twelve times that number might be saved. But how?

It all resulted from a marvel of detailed organisation. Already the Admiralty had with great prevision given notice that all privately owned motor craft of 30 to 100 feet in length were to be at their disposal. So, likewise, by means of a licensing system for all coasting vessels the Ministry of Shipping were kept aware of movements and could lay their hands on suitable vessels almost instantly.

The congregating of a vast improvised fleet numbering most of 1000 units therefore was just a matter of telephoning and telegraphing. Nothing like it had ever been devised. Trawlers, drifters, Thames sailing and motor barges, little cargo carriers, colliers, motorboats, motor yachts, many of the Royal National Lifeboats, open skiffs, oared boats from liners, sailing boats from Southend beach usually employed for pleasure parties, tugs from the Thames, even the six motor bawleys that gather up cockles from the estuary; pleasure paddle steamers accustomed to ply their trade along the Clyde, or to Llandudno, or Margate; one of the L.C.C. fireboats; steam yachts that were veterans when fighting U-boats in the last war; Dutch schooners and Belgian craft; swelled this extraordinary list till they numbered 665 in addition to the 222 naval units.

They were summoned from so far distant as the northeast and southwest coasts, but especially from the southeast areas. A new lifeboat, barely completed at an Essex river and never hitherto in service, joined the throng. Cross-channel steamers with ample passenger accommodation and high speed, normally carrying from seven to fourteen deck-hands, now received additional volunteers to man the boats which would have to be used as ferries from the beach.

One amateur yachtsman, assisted by his son, sailed his yacht all the way from Southampton to Dunkirk on his own initiative and fetched home a batch of tired soldiers. Another motor yacht had been lying hauled up ashore at Maidenhead; by magnificent enthusiasm she was launched, fitted out, engines overhauled, and sent towards London that same afternoon. Another yacht was lying in dock out of commission, but despite one of the lowest tides they forced her into the Thames and so across Channel.

When it was asked "How many soldiers will you be able to carry?", the owner replied — with exaggerated optimism — "Fifty, at a pinch". Actually she stowed 130 from Dunkirk jetty complete with their equipment.

The zeal on the part of all classes, suddenly kindled, was heart-moving. When it was known that our boys in Flanders had to be fetched afloat out of a perilous predicament, offers poured in pleading for acceptance, and those, who had to be declined, clamoured to be taken aboard anything.

One owner rang up the Admiralty and said:

"I understand you've commandeered my yacht?"

"Yes: I'm sorry, but ..."

"Oh, that's all right. There happens to be on board £30 worth of old brandy, and some champagne. I hope to goodness the boys find it."

Masters and crews of steamers responded to the call with universal spontaneity. Neither they nor the owners knew officially of what might happen the other side; of the sinkings and deaths and ceaseless risks. Yet the only black looks came when their offers could not always find selection.

And when still more crews were needed to replace those tottering with fatigue, the response could not have been more wonderful. In one factory where engineers were busy on Government work a sudden appeal was made for their services afloat.

"You'll be going into hell", they were told frankly, "you'll be bombed to blazes and machine-gunned too."

Without hesitating every one of these men threw down their tools, marched aboard ships they had never seen before, took over the engines, and twenty minutes later were sailing towards the inferno of Dunkirk.

Another engineering crowd in Harland & Wolff's works, London, were so keen to serve that they drove down to the coast in a charabanc and thought nothing of immediately tackling a seafaring job. Ancient mariners, too, forgot their years and placed their services only too gladly at their nation's disposal.

One old fellow, without consulting anybody, shoved off from the shore in his motorboat towing a number of open boats. Arrived in Dunkirk (having mercifully been able to avoid such items as minefields, bombs, shells, bullets) he did magnificent ferrying from beach to bigger ships, then at the last whilst helping others found himself left behind in the Dunkirk din and fury.

His boat had gone without him.

That would never do. So, leaping into the water, he swam for it, regained the motor craft and came home as if nothing out of the ordinary had been happening.

But now we must see the deeper thrills and tragedy that awaited.

And before we proceed further with the narrative we shall not forget the risks which at this time were being run by any ship which attempted during those final hours to enter Ostend. Of course history was repeating itself, some of us looked back on the days of that autumn 1914 when first Ostend had been a centre of future hope and then of the greatest anxiety to the Allies.

Towards the end of May, 1940, much was still thought in respect of that port, and we yet hoped to succour by supply ships the Army. That one of our vessels thus was destined to play a lone and forlorn part on such an occasion may be derived from the following report of the 689-tons "Aboukir" — one of the General Steam Navigation vessels — which has been written by her Master, Captain R. M. Woolfenden.

It is a remarkable document of great historical value. (The timing given is customary among mariners. Thus 8 p.m. = 20.00.):

"We cleared from Southampton on the afternoon of May 24th for the Downs for orders, arriving there in the morning of May 25th where we received orders to proceed to Ostend, to land supplies for the B.E.F., arriving off that port about 20.00 of the same day.

"The town was then in flames and the majority of the buildings on the sea front were in ruins, the quays and signal stations being absolutely deserted. The pilot boarded me when I was almost in my berth and informed me that apart from a few French Naval Officers there was no one of any authority in the port.

"I interviewed these Officers, who apparently had no knowledge of my ship, but suggested that I should start discharging at day-break.

"On the way back to the ship I met a British Army lorry driver, who told me that a Lieut. Harris with 38 British troops, who were adrift from their units, were standing by at a farm about five miles outside the town. We went out and brought them in, but on our arrival back at the ship we were bombed so intensely — the quay being the target — that I decided to abandon the ship until daylight. At 02.00 on May 26th I managed to get into telephone communication with the British Mission at Bruges, who instructed me to commence discharging, which I did with the assistance of the troops and the ship's crew. We were bombed off and on throughout the day. Later on the British Mission informed me that a British bomber had made a forced landing at Ostend, and would I try to make contact with her crew. Lieut. Harris and myself located these men at the Stane Aerodrome. After firing the machine, the two officers and two men who formed her crew joined my ship later on in the afternoon, bringing with them the machine-guns and instruments of the destroyed bomber. On the way back from the Aerodrome we picked up another 25 British troops who had also been separated from their units, also two wounded R.A.F. men.

"At 20.00 on the 26th May the bombing became so intense that once again we abandoned the ship until daybreak, resuming work with the assistance of Dutch Army deserters. Throughout the day German aircraft were continually bombing us, and at 15.00 they started dive bombing and machine gunning us so heavily that once again I decided to abandon the ship, having had two casualties, one being an R.A.F. gunner shot in the arm and a Belgian civilian shot in the left eye. Getting through to Bruges again, they instructed me to cease discharging and to load what Army vehicles I could, the rest to be destroyed; also the British Mission had decided to evacuate by my ship that night.

"I suggested sailing after dark at 22.00 to which they agreed. The Mission boarded me and at the stated time I cut my lines and sailed with approximately 220 people on board including crew, soldiers and Belgian refugees. I was followed out of the port by the British S.S. 'Marquis'. On clearing the entrance, enemy aircraft flew over dropping Verey lights and bombs. A call for assistance was sent out, as Mr. Newman of the British Mission had previously informed me that an escort consisting of two destroyers would be waiting for me off the port. This attack lasted for half an hour, when the aircraft returned to Ostend.

"Avoiding the regular channel, I steered direct for the North Goodwin Light Vessel hoping to miss any enemy craft that may have been waiting for me off the buoys. At 00.15 when approaching the North Hinder Buoy, I heard the second officer, Mr. Rust, give the order hard-a-starboard and I saw a torpedo crossing our course about 50 ft. ahead of the ship. The machine-gun was manned immediately by R.A.F. gunners whom I ordered to fire immediately on sighting the craft, while the ship's gunner, Church, was sent aft to stand by the smoke boxes. An S.O.S. was sent out and we commenced zig-zagging, no sign of the escort having appeared.

"About half an hour after the first attack we avoided a second torpedo which was fired from the port side and passed about 20 ft. astern, followed almost immediately by a third which also missed us. Five minutes after the third attack I sighted the enemy craft which turned out to be a coastal motor boat about 300 ft. on the port beam. The order was passed to the gunners to fire immediately they got the enemy on their sights, and I went hard-a-port to try and ram the craft. Our machine-gun got a burst of fire in, but the motor boat withheld her fire until we were about 150 ft. off her when she fired her fourth torpedo, which I was unable to avoid being so close. This torpedo struck us at an angle underneath the bridge on the port side.

"The concussion was terrific, and I had a vague idea of the bridge collapsing and finding myself down the fore hold; fortunately floating out and clear when the ship settled by the head. After the ship had foundered, which I reckon she did in a minute and a half, the C.M.B. turned her searchlight on us and machine-gunned us. There must have been quite a few killed then.

"At daybreak three or four ships passed us without seeing us, but at 07.00 a Flotilla of H.M. destroyers picked us up. The kind treatment we received on board is beyond all praise.

"As you can see from this report, there was no time to lower the boats, but A.B. Carrol managed to slip one of the life rafts which was later on filled by Belgian refugees. This raft I regret to say received the brunt of enemy machine-gun fire, wiping out nearly all the occupants.

"As to what caused the death of the Chief Officer, I am unable to say. He appeared to be all right after the action as I was speaking to him in the water, but did not see him after daylight.

"I would like to say a word in praise of my officers and crew. Throughout the intense bombing in Ostend they carried out their work with extreme coolness and cheerfulness, and during the three-quarters of an hour engagement with the C.M.B. there was at no time any sign of panic. I would like to mention in particular L. Tanner, sailor, who was at the wheel during the engagement. Although only a lad of barely 19 years of age, he carried out my orders with precision and coolness.

"I would like to add that after the first torpedo attack I sent orders aft to release the smoke box, in the hope of losing the enemy craft but, for some unknown reason, this order was never carried out."

CHAPTER V — THE ANSWER TO THE CRISIS

IMMEDIATELY before the German invasion towards the coast, there were still five ports on which to fall back, and through which we still expected to pass supplies towards France and the Low Countries. These were, respectively, Zeebrugge, Ostend, Dunkirk, Calais, and Boulogne. We have in due course seen that Zeebrugge was effectively blocked by the sinking of our concrete-filled ships; the sea-gates of the Bruges canal with the lock-working mechanism demolished, and the lock approach filled up.

We have just remarked how Ostend had to be left in a hurry, how Calais and Boulogne after strong resistance fell into German hands, and this left Dunkirk alone as the gate through which the threatened B.E.F. was to pass if it meant to reach England alive. The original stretch of beach selected extended for eight or nine miles eastward from Dunkirk past the Bray Dunes towards La Panne, which is near Zuydcoote village that gives its name to the Zuydcoote Pass presently to be mentioned. The latter channel is much subject to change (as ships learned to their cost), and it is well to wait till the tide has risen. Moreover, care has to be taken, especially by night, that the strong stream does not set the vessel athwart her course.

Off La Panne itself the east-going, or flood, stream makes at about 3 hours before local High Water during 6 hours, and there is very little slack tide. This had to be borne in mind by the barges and other of the vessels sending boats or placing themselves ashore. Really it was far from an easy beach, because the distance from High Water mark to the nearest point where most ships laid at anchor measured a half to three-quarters of a mile. And of course there could be no sort of cover for troops waiting on the beach. Yet these were to queue up with as much orderliness as if at a booking office of a railway station.

We must remember that from virtually Calais onwards to La Panne the dunes were swept by shell-fire, whilst from skywards the Nazi aeroplanes rained death by bullets and bombs. Because of this realisation no withdrawal from that neighbourhood could be a picnic, but (as we just now hinted) it was well ahead perceived on May 14, by the Admiralty, that many small vessels of 30 to 100 feet in length would almost certainly be required somewhere along the sandy shores. The announcement of the compulsory registration, which included especially yachts known as motor cruisers, was made both in the Press and on the wireless. The date is significant as showing that it was perceived the trend of affairs must end only at the sea, and that the Admiralty authorities well realised what was coming.

Five days later, on Sunday evening, May 19, a most urgent request was made by the Admiralty to the Ministry of Shipping for very many "degaussed" (i.e. protected against magnetic mines) coasting vessels to proceed for the Downs and there await orders of the Vice-Admiral Commanding Dover. This, be it recollected, was the day after the enemy had broken through the line around Sedan, overwhelming the French.

By means of a system of licensing, under which all vessels engaged in coastal and short sea voyages are controlled through the Ministry of Shipping, the movements of these units were well known. Thus, as we saw, the Ministry could instantly lay its hands on all suitable craft, and within two hours of the Admiralty's request most of the ships had been sent to the Downs. By Monday afternoon, when Weygand had been appointed Commander-in-Chief to succeed Gamelin, all available vessels under that control were ready. By the efficient organisation of these two departments the Army was therefore assured of considerable help from non-naval vessels.

Owners were not actually told the purpose for which their vessels were needed, but it was obvious from the enthusiastic response that they fully understood the desperate duties about to begin. In the disappointment exhibited by those not immediately reckoned suitable for the occasion, it was also clear that owners and crews were prepared to do their very best.

Now, about the time of Holland's invasion, many of those Dutch motor coasters had sought shelter in our ports, so the Netherlands Shipping Committee, acting on these owners' behalf, agreed to place such vessels at the Ministry's disposal. Being of light draught and handy size (500 to 1000 tons), it was believed that the motor coasters would prove suitable for any evacuation. The Dover Flag Officer in Charge, known to us all now as Vice-Admiral Sir Bertram Ramsay, was approached and verified the probable utility. That is why presently were to be seen H.M. "Skoots" flying the White Ensign at the stern, for British naval officers and ratings replaced the original crews. Altogether a fleet of 42 Dutch vessels were to be ready for the fray.

To give some idea of the magnitude of the Ministry's task, it may be mentioned that — leaving out the yachts and such-like smaller numbers — there were 91 Master Mariners chosen for this evacuation, and of that number 57 were commanding passenger and store ships while 34 were tugmasters, but more than 600 smaller vessels also took part.

When the withdrawal of more than 335,000 soldiers was, on Sunday, May 26, inaugurated under Admiral Ramsay, neither he nor anyone else had the slightest hope that it would develop into the vast success which followed after the prayers of many people that day. All the available ships were sent from Dover, together with a score of naval officers and some 180 ratings. They had no idea — officially at least — for what mission these were being sent, but on the way towards Dunkirk the many bombs intimated what might be expected. The whole control of this daring affair was really part of "The Dynamo Room", which gave its name to the undertaking generally, though it was precisely a highly busy place at Dover with seven telephones always buzzing and sixteen persons always on the job.

The main idea, initially, was within forty-eight hours to rescue and send back to England the greatest number possible, and Captain Denny from his experience in such an operation within Norwegian waters possessed practical knowledge of such a difficult affair. Matters, however, so well progressed that after two days this might become a far bigger show than had been contemplated. Not a mere 10 per cent, but hundreds of thousands. Not only the B.E.F., but many French soldiers as well.

That Dunkirk was afire, and the docks a shambles, could not be deemed encouraging, and the heat was so great that the only portion where a ship could go alongside was the couple of narrow breakwaters supported by wooden piles. No one had supposed that 250,000 would eventually embark from there, or that most of 100,000 would come off from the beaches. It was the inspiration of naval officers which guided the ships and the soldiers to the ships. No matter that gangways were impossible. Did not narrow mess-tables do as well, even if it was mighty difficult for men, crossing in the darkness, already tottering with fatigue?

When you think of it, it seems incredible that an essentially naval proceeding such as Dunkirk should be carried out chiefly by civilians; that many of them in the smaller units came over and acted on their own initiative. As things grew busier we realised the need of those 34 motor-boats and the 881 ship's boats collected and sent across from the Port of London Authority.

"Our peak day," afterwards said Admiral Ramsay, "was 66,000 men taken off, but at the expense of casualties to our craft." The enemy having mounted big batteries commanding the direct route, which passed near Calais, we had to adopt new routes so that instead of a round journey being 76 miles, this became lengthened to 175; but then the Germans replied by bringing up batteries to command that way, so we had to find a third, viz. across sand-banks which first had to be cleared by the minesweepers.

Boulogne had been evacuated by six of our destroyers doing some smart work between 5-30 p.m. and 3 a.m., and in spite of the fierce fire they took away 4600 soldiers, though we lost the Captain in charge of this flotilla, being sniped and shot whilst on the bridge. Troops had gallantly held on to Calais till it became untenable, and shells from the shore were too much for our ships.

But Dunkirk was something on a bigger scale. Just as the sixteen people in "The Dynamo Room" at Dover became so tired after the first three or four days that they lay down asleep in their chairs or on the floor, before waking up and resuming work, so after a couple of days all our landing parties at Dunkirk became so exhausted from lack of sleep that another hundred men had to be despatched.

On the first night we got 13,000 soldiers away, on May 27 we sent off 20,000, but on the Tuesday we reached 45,000. That was why the Admiralty were asked to send every craft possible within twenty-four hours. Thus the second phase begins with the hordes of these comparative midgets, and as one was sunk or abandoned the crews took over others. Because on Thursday, May 30, the weather conditions were unfavourable, there was a marked decrease in aerial activity; though after the enemy brought up still more batteries it became impossible to continue evacuating by daylight, and the peak necessarily dropped from 66,000 to 30,000 *per diem*. The Admiral considered truly that, only by the extraordinarily fine ship-handling and the amazing endurance of men, was the job done at all. The pity is that so many of the small vessels, which disappeared into the Dunkirk haze, left no record behind them and will never receive the thanks due to them.

Nowadays, what with high-powered speedboats and destroyers, Dover is no great distance from Dunkirk, so that it was possible for the Admiral to maintain intimate knowledge of what was being done amid French waters; and as he raced athwart the Straits there met him that awed spectacle of fires and black smoke westward of the harbour, where oil refineries and storage had been situated. Ten miles of sandy beach! But how overcast and dark it all seemed until dawn off La Panne, and beyond, showed the sands black to the waterline with soldiers about to go home. It would soon be their turn to enter the boats, but frankly on the Wednesday (May 29), it seemed that of the thousands only a fraction could be sent off in those few boats to the ships waiting hard by.

Yet most wonderful that, almost as soon as asked for, there came from England both pulling and power boats: it seemed as if the prayers of Sunday were being answered by a miracle. The low clouds, poor visibility, little wind and calm sea, were ideal for bringing off troops, though the considerable surf breaking on the sands made this inshore boatwork difficult. One of the hardest tasks was, having filled up the open boats and placed their human contents aboard some destroyer in the offing, to get the empty ones back for a new load; though some soldiers were so expert at boatmanship that many times they went backwards and forwards like a ferry.

Those barricades of discarded tanks and lorries thrown across the beach down to Low Water mark, both at Bray and La Panne, were certainly a bright idea. Off the former place the Royal Engineers did a fine bit of inventiveness making a plank footway with handrail support along the top, so that the men could walk out along this improvised pier to the boats coming alongside and thus were saved from a longer row. It was a convenience that, at certain states of the tide, motorboats might come alongside so easily; and out of this notion it could be but a gradual step towards the use of sailing barges as pontoons.

When the fresh northerly wind on Friday sent a heavy sea on to the dunes, troops were induced rather towards Dunkirk and we thus tried to embark so many as possible therefrom; for with those gradually shelving sands it needed on an average most of six hours to fill up a destroyer with her quota of 1200 men, and that was too long when bombing made everything hideous. Most especially bad weather at High Tide that forenoon (about 8 a.m.) interfered with work, and the stranding of several craft on the falling tide did not help matters.

Around noon the enemy from his eastern shore batteries shelled La Panne and made it practically untenable, for a Nazi balloon was up observing from east of this place spotting on behalf of the gunners. A terrific aerial battle ensued also, and it looked as if our fighters aloft were greatly outnumbered. Thus were ships and beaches attacked viciously.

On Friday the enemy came further west in the afternoon with his shells. It will be related in another chapter how, off Bray on May 29, the S.S. "Clan Macalister" had been abandoned, but she was still burning on the last day of this month and the enemy perpetually directed missiles into her as well as on other wrecks. This became one of the most noticeable features of German mentality off Dunkirk: a wrecked and abandoned vessel being an irresistible invitation for assault. But the enemy likewise hit H.M.S. "Vivacious", a 1000 tons destroyer.

On this last evening of the month General Lord Gort and his staff embarked for England, but if it was symbolical that the greater portion of evacuating had passed, this did not by any means infer that excitement and difficulty were gone. Heavy fire persisted from the shore batteries throughout that night off La Panne, dying down only at dawn when it was succeeded by the aircraft. The defence line had been withdrawn a little further west till it lay between La Panne and Bray, for which reason ships had to be more in the direction of Dunkirk, so that La Panne's beaches which had begun so badly were now utterly deserted.

Sunday morning, June 1, began a hard day, with the enemy bombers reappearing escorted by strong fighter patrols. Our destroyers were having a fierce time when H.M.S. "Keith" (Captain E. L. Berthon, R.N., a D.S.C. of the last war) was attacked at 7-45 a.m. by a dozen Junkers which flew horizontally to a spot about 9000 feet above their object, then dived directly till some 2000 feet and released their missiles. Although these happily missed the 1400 tons flotilla leader, they fell so close to H.M.S. "Hebe", an 835 tons minesweeper, as to jam her rudder and sink H.M.S. "Havant" (Lieut.-Commander A. F. Burnell-Nugent, R.N.) near to Dunkirk; whilst H.M.S. "Skipjack" (Lieut.-Commander F. B. Proudfoot, R.N.), an 815 tons Fleet Minesweeper, was likewise sent to the bottom. Just after 8 a.m. the "Keith" was struck by a salvo whilst rushing at high speed. Up went a roar of steam — for she developed 34,000 horse power with her turbines — and began to list.

It was an impressive sound and sight, as through after funnel and boiler-room casing the released steam hissed its freedom, and she was anchored in the fairway; but the list to port increased as badly as 20 degrees, only about a couple of feet freeboard remained above water-line, yet still she was undaunted. Two tugs stood by her, when yet another determined attack brought a hit in the forward boiler-room. She had to be abandoned, many of the ship's company, including the Captain, transferring to a tug.

The onslaught against our Motor Torpedo Boats was met by dodging at highest speed the falling bombs, but H.M.S. "Basilisk", another destroyer of 1360 tons "owned" by Commander M. Richmond, R.N., was sunk about the same time by a high-flying bomber. These, then, must be added to the losses already of the three destroyers "Grafton", "Grenade" and "Wakeful".

Inevitable was the Admiral's decision during this Saturday that further operations must be confined to the cover of night; but innumerable paddlers, tugs, and small vessels were fetching troops away from the piers and the lighter craft kept bringing from Dunkirk dunes across the strong tide many soldiers which had to be put aboard ships lying 1½ miles off. Luckily it was a very calm evening, with only a soft southerly air which drifted lazily the huge cloud of smoke over harbour and sands. Thus against the aerial attacks was provided a protection which scarcely interfered with the ground visibility down below.

An amazing picture it all presented as night descended that Saturday. The eastern arm of Dunkirk silhouetted by the large flames behind, and the never-ending stream of weary men moving in a seaward direction. Sometimes they broke into a tired run, more frequently they just plodded blindly towards the steamers, at other times they were packed as stationary humanity along the narrow parapet waiting their turn for the next ship to berth.

Have we seemed to stress unduly this physical weariness? These men on the final days were those who had borne the brunt of fighting and as the B.E.F.'s rearguard could still, after three weeks of continuous battling, march in perfect order to those jetties. Furthermore they were cheery-hearted and could sing. Veritable heroes of Dunkirk were these soldiers who, during the night of June 1-2 (followed on the next two nights by the finest of French troops), defended the place and made this astounding evacuation, not of hundreds but of thousands, practicable.

Shelling of harbours, of piers, of beaches, of ships lying off, were characteristic of tonight, but curiously the piers still stood even if a trawler was sunk in the harbour. It seemed incredible that over a narrow 5-foot wooden planking so many tens of thousands stepped to safety, so that now only a handful of the B.E.F. remained to be despatched.

Yet the enemy's approach could not be much longer delayed. There would not remain many more hours for this tremendous adventure that had originally seemed so desperate. The night of Sunday-Monday (June 2-3) was atmospherically beautiful, with a clear and unclouded sky and a fresh northerly wind. High Water was to be about 10-45 p.m., but one-and-a-half hours earlier arrived from England additional motorboats sent for regulating the traffic. They were unfortunate enough to receive the enemy's bitterest attentions on passage.

Unless we had been a nation of seafarers, this Dunkirk evacuation would have been utterly impossible: we were asking officers of the Royal and Merchant Navies to do the most difficult things with their vessels in a confined and busy space. Berthing on a flood tide with a northerly wind blowing was always a trial to the ablest handler of ships, even when tugs were ready to assist: yet we shall learn from other chapters this was accomplished because we owned the right personnel. It cannot be too heavily underlined that the soldiers would unquestionably have been delivered to captivity or death, except for sailors' brilliant contending against the most obstinate conditions.

So before dawn broke on Monday, June 3, almost the last contingent of the B.E.F. was embarked: only 500 wounded to come off in a hospital ship, and she of course was to be bombed and sunk by a savage enemy. Oh, yes: there were tense moments and thrilling hours to the very end. Just when the tide had begun to fall, the French S.S. "Rouen" had the misfortune to drift on to the sandy part of the western harbour. Attempts to refloat her were unavailing, and at Low Water she lay a pathetic picture of immobility.

Yet, with the return of a flooding tide, she did get off and that day reached Dover.

French troops in numbers had to be withdrawn from immediate embarking, because the enemy was attacking heavily and a strong counter-attack developed. That was why about half the shipping on the 3rd had to leave without a full complement, but by 2-45 a.m. troops again were coming on to the jetties. A fine, clear sky with a fresh northerly wind looked down on the concluding incidents, to a harbour congested with French fishing vessels and other small fry which were impeding the bigger ships. That gallant French Admiral Abrial, who had commanded the port of Dunkirk till the very end, came aboard one of the last departing vessels for England, and the final ship sailed just after 3 a.m. Ten minutes later the block ships arrived that were to render Dunkirk useless for some time to the Germans.

Only the very few indeed remained ashore, but the enemy had so far advanced that he was machine-gunning the piers. The greatest withdrawal of all time had ended, and when once back in Britain these harassed soldiers could be reconstituted for other tasks.

CHAPTER VI — HOW THE PORT OF LONDON HELPED

QUITE early in the proceedings it came about that the Port of London Authority was able to assist the Royal Navy in many different ways, and by means of the former's vast domain there was an organisation in readiness, well arranged for such a crisis, waiting only the order to begin.

Did coal-burning craft require considerable quantities of fuel? These were sent down to Margate for immediate stocks, having been towed down the river. Was it feared that our troops in France would be very short of drinking water? Then so many clean petrol cans were steamed out and placed full aboard suitable vessels. Were boats, such as the P. & O. type measuring 27 ft. long and 10 ft. wide, required for pulling purposes, or Orient Line motorboats, such had only to be collected and despatched.

The idea of employing comparatively small wooden barges was suggested on May 27, and as a first step a list by the P.L.A. grew into being comprising those sailing and auxiliary units which traded up and down the Thames and Medway already awaiting orders to load. Between fifty and sixty of such craft were on this date at various parts of the Thames, the docks, and the lower reaches of the Medway. A 'fleet in being' could thus be counted on.

But at first the Admiralty did not favourably consider this suggestion, wherefore on the Tuesday most of these ships resumed their loading for coastwise ports.

Then on Wednesday the Admiralty returned to the matter, and asked for 21 wooden barges of the sailing type and such shallow draught that they could be used over the sandbanks to the Dunkirk beach. Barely was the demand expressed than the barges were collected and sent down to Tilbury during this Wednesday, steel helmets provided for the crews, an issue of money supplied to the latter for expenses, whilst drinking water and rations were immediately forthcoming. After that it was only a matter of towing craft round by tugs from Tilbury to the Downs and Dover.

Could the Germans with all their reputed thoroughness and scheduling have achieved so much in a few brief hours? It matters not that ultimately 16 were at Dover selected for service, but there were many more ready to be taken by the seagoing tugs "Crested Cock", "Ocean Cock", "Cervia", "Sun XI" and "Sun XII." It was the P.L.A.'s Assistant Harbour Master in the Thames' Upper District who supervised the rounding up of these sailing barges and despatching them by tugs to Tilbury, and it was he who supervised the most necessary and valuable assemblage in King George V Dock of the 130 ship's boats owned by various lines. By working all day and overtime the Authority's steam and motor launches compelled them to come in. Captain Lovell in the launch "Nore" spent the busiest time, and had the Admiralty so resolved the P.L.A. could have placed at their disposal not less than 75 sailing barges.

In another chapter we are able to witness the adventures and adversities which the latter species of vessel was to encounter, but the message sent by the Admiralty to the P.L.A. at 10-15 a.m. of May 29 was of such an urgent nature that many of the craft were literally fetched from their moorings; food so quickly obtained from the Tilbury Hotel that the first three were able to start off for Ramsgate by 5-15 p.m. and then 31 sailing barges got away by midnight.

It was interesting to note some of the details in this collection. The P.L.A. tug "Darent" spent eight hours on the 29th, and toiled till late at night of the 30th, on the following day towing four barges from Beckton laden with coal for Margate which in turn was for the naval force. One firm — Messrs. Clements, Knowling & Co. Ltd., of Brentford — were given orders to drop all tows on the Thames, and the tugs "Diana" with "Scorcher" were to proceed collecting any of these barges moored between Brentford and the Tower Pier.

Similar arrangements dealt with the four sections of the river:

(1) Tower Bridge to Erith.
(2) Erith to Purfleet.
(3) Purfleet to Lower Hope Point.
(4) Lower Hope Point to Chapman Light.

It was with the goodwill of various firms that this was possible. Whilst the P.L.A. was scouring its Dock system, the Lower Thames and Medway, the Thames Conservancy reported the names of light craft in their jurisdiction, and the Lee Conservancy did likewise. The Shell Mex company sent stores of lubricating and fuel oil, but the thousands of two-gallon cans obtained from them and the Petroleum Board, filled with drinking water, were much esteemed. The barge crews were given £5 apiece danger money, plus £2 ahead for likely expenses, and this money they were later allowed to keep as gratuity.

Of course no little difficulty was experienced in gathering together all sorts of rowing boats. Many of them had lain in store for months and immediately leaked when launched into the docks, but the wreck raising vessel "King Lear" was engaged in righting and pumping certain of these in Tilbury Basin. Incidentally it may be mentioned that a great deal of work for such tugs as the "John Hawkins" or Messrs. Gaselee's "Gnat" and "Wasp" was needed in returning those boats which could not be employed. It was this company's tugs which also brought 82 boats and 15 sailing barges to Tilbury, 16 launches to Southend and Sheerness, and 14 motor launches to Ramsgate.

Altogether the amount of work in docking and undocking was terrific. In Tilbury alone 21 ship's boats had to be lifted from quay to water by a floating derrick. Some of the craft were destined never to see their owners again, some boats after excellently sharing in the evacuation came back unidentifiable, many were cast away, others were accepted as replacements, but the whole colossal scheme required a vast amount of effort merely in the sorting out. As a slight idea of this may be mentioned that the P.L.A. undocked over 200 of these boats, many sailing barges, and afterwards redocked them; that after the small motor cruisers and the like returned from Dunkirk, Messrs. Tough of Teddington on June 9 towed by their tug 21 from Sheerness, and 30 were fetched by scratch crews, though it took weeks collecting from different parts of the coast other odds and ends.

On the Upper Thames there are to be found, for many miles, light draught motor yachts of all kinds, which during any normal spring and summer would be afloat in commission; for the growth of what are known as 'cabin cruisers' since the last war has been one of the most striking features along these fresh waters. Because of the war, however, comparatively few remained in use, but many were lying laid up ashore.

It was believed that careful selection from such a fleet of small craft between 30 ft. and 100 ft. long, with a draught of less than 4 ft. might prove of considerable utility for transferring soldiers from shallow beaches, though obviously accommodation would suffice for only few passengers at a time. The technique would differ from that of the destroyers, sloops, trawlers, drifters, and cargo vessels: whereas the former, after loading up, could hurry away direct for home, these small motor yachts — with a few exceptions — must act as feeders, or ferryboats bringing off from the shore relays to the shipping anchored in the Roads.

But the problem immediately arose of how this summer fleet could be collected from their winter-quarters, launched, fitted out, and sent down river below locks to the Thames in its tidal reaches.

Wisely the decision arrived at was to make use of expert knowledge and centralisation. The firm selected for this purpose was Messrs. Tough Bros., Boat Builders, of Teddington, where the tidal Thames ends, and from above this lock right away almost to Oxford such powered yachts might be found — if not hauled ashore, at least tethered in some secluded backwater.

Of course it was by no means an easy job, for whilst legal authority existed for borrowing yacht-owners' property, some of the craft were quite unsuited to cross the sea, others would need considerable preliminary attention before their motors reached a state of reliability. Therefore the only thing was to eliminate all correspondence and red-tape, allow the selector widest scope for judgement, but above all things push the matter through to its finality in the shortest possible time.

When at 10-30 a.m. of Monday, May 27, the Small Vessels Pool telephoned Teddington, this special and sudden method of acquiring flotillas was set going with tremendous impetus. Everything worked smoothly but with celerity, an officer arrived from the Admiralty to inspect, and fourteen boats were immediately selected. Twelve hours later, by a triumph of energetic efficiency, all these had been made ready for sea, fuelled, and by 6 a.m. of Tuesday, May 28, they were on their way with scratch crews obtained chiefly from Messrs. Tough's yard. Thus in less than twenty hours from the first suggestion, an abstract idea became a living reality.

Spectators who had no official knowledge of what was happening were impressed by this strange procession down river and made a shrewd guess as to their purpose. Arrived at Sheerness Dockyard, where all was bustle and intense activity, these little craft were assigned volunteer crews whilst the others reluctantly went back to set about providing still more yachts. The spirit of adventure seized everyone so determinedly that it was difficult to resist the invitation for an exciting but vaguely inferred project. With much heartburning it seemed more desirable for the national good that the Teddington crews should hurry on with a further collecting rather than proceed to Dunkirk and leave nobody to deliver a second batch.

On Wednesday the demand for more was met by similar direct action. Mr. D. A. Tough proceeded up river with an officer requisitioning suitable motor cruisers wherever to be found, and the Admiralty agreed on making Teddington the port of assembly. The whole thing became so quickly organised that no time could be wasted in notifying owners beforehand, so in many cases these gentlemen received the first intimation only when they saw their moorings empty.

By this date the Dunkirk operations had so developed that a higher optimism suggested much more extensive withdrawals than originally had seemed possible. An appeal for volunteer mariners was sent out on the wireless, applications came in by telephone, yachtsmen offered their services, and members of the Port of London River Emergency Service were sent up to Teddington to act as runner crews.

It was a great disappointment for the latter that only a few were allowed to take their craft over towards Dunkirk, but as an integral part of the Home Defence system they could not be spared. All the same they were able to render valuable help by piloting many pleasure vessels and private yachts into the Thames lower reaches, assisting at Tilbury in the fuelling and provisioning; but eleven of these R.E.S. volunteers did manage to go across after all.

At the Teddington yard, where every man was working to the fullest limit, it all seemed like one human powerhouse of electricity. Patriotism and a personal interest inspired these efforts simultaneously: not merely was the national army in danger but among the B.E.F. were several men who till conscripted had been employed here. So handsomely did employers and workers unite their efforts that by Friday over 100 small vessels had been sent on their way. Thus to the fleets of barges and pleasure steamers, coasters and cargo carriers, was now added that of motor yachts and launches.

Time plays strange antics with ships and men. Many people will remember the 23,000 tons German battlecruiser "Moltke" in the last war. Among other undertakings she played her part in the Gorleston Raid of November, 1914. Well, it so happened that in course of time after Armistice the German Admiral's barge became a British motor yacht and was named "Count Dracula"; for "Moltke" sank herself at Scapa Flow on June 21, 1919. Twenty-one years passed, and the "Count Dracula" went over to "the other side" and helped at Dunkirk in the rescue of British soldiers from the Germans.

So also in the last war there was a certain M.L. which, after flying the White Ensign and being sold out of the service, became converted by Messrs. Tough into a pleasure vessel and under the name of "Tigris" made daily excursions up the Thames from Richmond. A funnel was added to get rid of the exhaust gases. Now the "Tigris" found herself again amid hostilities after many years, and with her own river crew not merely proceeded to Dunkirk but made three separate trips and saved about 900 men.

That in itself was a new exciting chapter in her biography, nor did things end thus. The crisis came when in a sinking condition she had to be abandoned, but, lest "Tigris" should fall into the enemy's hands, the crew dismantled her water pump. Two days passed and she was sighted off the Goodwins with 90 Frenchmen aboard. One of them, being mechanically minded, had cleverly adapted the bilge pump to serve instead of the circulating pump, so that now in British waters she was soon towed inside Ramsgate Harbour. I saw "Tigris" again at Teddington shortly after her return. Some of her glass windows had been smashed and an ominous bullet hole in the funnel told how close to death she passed: yet, otherwise, she seemed little different from the excursion vessel that used to glide past peaceful lawns and beneath stone bridges.

There never was a more miscellaneous and unusual congregation of craft than those which appeared in front of Dunkirk. Apart from "Tigris" there were light up-river steamers whose 3-ft. draught made them less safe in a seaway than among the water-lilies. As one looks back, it still seems scarcely credible that so many frail bits of shipping dared to tempt the open sea and invite attack from explosives. Quite a number were lost by enemy action, or had to be abandoned because of accident, or again through engine-room breakdown. Perhaps at the time it appeared heartless to cast away such valuable pieces of property after the crew had been saved; but it was a ruthless occasion when every ship and every human being were working against the clock. Even to spend a few hours at sea making adjustments, doing a few repairs that would ordinarily have been effected when fitting out for the summer season, could not be considered.

The yacht must continue to go ahead or be abandoned.

Extravagantly fantastic this pageant of sea-power must have appeared at any selected moment. But was there possible a more amazing variety, a more representative marine effort on behalf of our land fighters? We have left for posterity a chapter of history which succeeding generations may well envy; we have made the most glorious pages of the past seem commonplace. As an example of the all-pull-together-on-the-same-rope principle, this Dunkirk effort was the most democratic sort of co-operation attempted afloat, and the most gigantic display of tonnage.

Only a great maritime nation could have staged such a first-class show, yet hardly one type of vessel was unrepresented. Among our obsolescent rigs, for instance, is the Thames estuary bawley, of which only a handful survive. With her boomless mainsail, its brails, and long gaff, this fast and handy type is exactly suited for dodging in and out amongst the shoals and sandbanks where the seas are often short, steep, hollow.

Some go shrimping from Gravesend, others go cockling from Leigh, and nowadays the custom is to have auxiliary motors. It would be difficult to imagine any ship-type, any sort of fishing vessel, less likely to be used in naval operations, though that did not prevent them from going across to Dunkirk. True, their comparatively deep draught made them far from ideal for those gradually shelving beaches, but such a detail did not restrain the gallant enterprise of their hardy personnel. At least one plucky skipper and crew paid for this devotion with their lives.

We all are familiar with those comic drawings, which the weekly papers publish from time to time, concerning seasick trippers going for a sail in the local "Skylark." Perhaps not everyone is aware that the prototype belongs to Brighton beach, though we should no more have associated this than the bawley type for warlike activities.

To be precise, Brighton can boast of "Skylark I", "Skylark II", "Skylark III" and "Skylark IV", all fitted with auxiliary motors and each having a crew of two, three, or five men. This beach flotilla was launched by willing helpers, three "Skylarks" leaving on May 30, and one early the next day; but you can well understand that when British soldiers — accustomed to many surprises of all sorts — discovered at Dunkirk that in real earnest and not for a joke they were being taken off by one of the most popular institutions of our social life, it was agreed that this could be a funny old war no matter how seriously some might regard it.

Perhaps not the least interesting feature was that crews were found, that the "Skylark" helpers summoned men for expediting departure; fuel and provisions were put aboard, boats despatched — all at short notice within a few hours because the local Resident Naval Officer, the Beach Inspector, and Brighton Police worked together as one man for one big cause.

Some people after examining photographs and artists' sketches have wondered how and whence certain large motor launches got to Dunkirk. The answer is that these in peace time were carried by luxury-cruise liners for taking passengers ashore at some Adriatic port or within a Norwegian fjord. Most of these steamers being now employed in His Majesty's Navy, the launches had been put away in the stores of Thames docks, but when Dunkirk clamoured its demands, derricks hauled the launches afloat, caulkers tightened leaky seams, and away went these craft again seaworthy.

CHAPTER VII — THE TASK FOR SEAFARERS

IT was the urgency of Dunkirk which demanded employment of the most unusual vessels. "Anything capable of keeping afloat and carrying troops across the Channel": that was the only thing which mattered.

One could scarcely have imagined for passenger transport a type of vessel less suitable than the Thames "sludge hoppers",[2] yet one of these (owned by the Tilbury Contracting & Dredging Co.) went over and in one trip fetched no fewer than 487 soldiers. Even the Isle of Wight ferryboat "Fishbourne", which normally runs across from Portsmouth, was summoned into the Great Evacuation scheme, and we need not envy the task imposed on anxious tugmasters by such exceptional service.

Take the case of those three tugs, "Duke", "Prince", and "Princess", offered by their owners, Messrs. Samuel Williams & Sons. Having left Dagenham on May 31, called at Southend thence and brought sailing barges round the North Foreland to the Downs below Ramsgate, these little steamers left their charges at anchor and next forenoon started towing the "Fishbourne" towards France.

An awkward, harassing job from the first, and after two hours' progress the starboard rope of "Princess" carried away in the swell. About the same time four sailing barges, towed by the well-known steam tug "Sun III", had also set out, but after another hour and a half this little flotilla was missing, whereupon the "Duke" turned back to seek them.

After a while, contact having been made, the "Duke" took over from "Sun III" the sailing barge "Haste-Away", but because of the bad visibility soon lost sight of the "Fishbourne" contingent. Then another sailing barge, "Ada Mary", twice broke adrift from "Sun III", so "Duke's" Captain decided to take her in tow likewise.

All was going now quite nicely, five hours had passed since leaving the Downs, and Dunkirk lay some couple of miles to the southward. Suddenly at 2-40 p.m. a violent air raid broke over the "Duke" like a thunderstorm, bombs dropped off her starboard side and she would have been sunk had not British fighter 'planes swept against the enemy and split up the Nazi formation.

But a short while later "Duke" was to sight one result of this aerial combat. A lifeboat containing forty British soldiers and one naval rating came into view; survivors from a sunken ship. Twenty of these were picked up by "Duke", and the other half taken aboard "Sun III".

The complexion of things looked ugly, nor was it improved by immediate consideration. An officer in charge of the soldiers regarded with dismay the general outlook, but the exact whereabouts of Dunkirk could not be located amid that pall of smoke from burning oil-tanks. Also, having lost contact with the "Prince" and "Princess", the "Duke" could not be certain of the correct route. She therefore steamed about for an hour, and finally followed "Sun III".

The spring afternoon was waning, anything might happen now, the danger zone had been thoroughly entered; at 4-20 p.m. "Duke" sighted another lifeboat containing eleven British sailors and a Midshipman. They were survivors from H.M.S "Basilisk", a destroyer, sunk off Dunkirk in an air raid. Having taken this dozen on board, and secured the boat astern from one of the barges, the tug might have believed that the voyage would become normal.

Not a bit!

Only three-quarters of an hour intervened, and two aircraft began circling round. This time they were unmistakably British and commenced signalling.

"Steer south," was the message read.

So "Duke" obeyed, followed also by "Sun III", and before long they were thus led to where another couple of lifeboats loomed up and another dozen men from shipwreck found salvation. Altogether the voyage of those four tugs failed in its original purpose, since "Prince" and "Princess" brought "Fishbourne" no nearer to Dunkirk than two miles distant when a naval officer "told us to turn round and get away home as soon as possible." Both "Duke" and "Sun III" also were compelled to return, and all of them were back off Ramsgate by 7-30 a.m. of June 2.

The Germans had made the beaches too unhealthy for evacuation work.

Certainly that night of Saturday-Sunday (June 1-2) showed the enemy doing his utmost, and venting his fury against our ships. To the Germans it was extremely annoying that of the Anglo-French Armies which had been regarded as about to suffer annihilation already so many thousands were safely transported beyond the Nazis' reach.

Yet the evacuation was not yet completed, the German troops had still to enter Dunkirk, and meanwhile every sort and variety of vessel continued to be rushed over from England. These tugs were being required all the time, and for all sorts of purposes, so on Saturday evening the tug "Fossa" was despatched from Ramsgate towing a yacht.

She reached Dunkirk at 1 a.m., berthed alongside the breakwater whence more than a hundred soldiers — chiefly French and Belgian — poured aboard, and by 2 a.m. "Fossa" started back for Ramsgate, this time with a couple of yachts in tow. She had therefore wasted not one minute on the job.

The night was calm but very dark, the sea in a kindly mood, but what with the absence of lights and the vast amount of traffic dashing furiously hither and thither, dodging each other no less than the enemy's explosives, every navigator's life was akin to a mad medley. The churning of water by destroyers' propellers, the sudden loom of some transport at anchor in the Roads, the thrashing of some ex-pleasure steamer's paddle-wheels, the quick darting of motor-launches from the shadow of a trawler — it was really wonderful that so few collisions actually occurred, and that so many narrow escapes were rendered possible.

Now the "Fossa", like any other tug, was extremely handy, but in trying to work her way through the narrow channel the task became scarcely possible. One after another the naval vessels sped by to enter between Dunkirk's breakwaters, but "Fossa's" position was similar to that of a child trying to cross Piccadilly Circus against the flow of traffic at the time when theatres are emptying. And, in avoiding these moving dangers, "Fossa" grounded badly on a sandbank.

To make matters worse, the tide was still falling. So what?

A hundred soldiers in jeopardy? That was the real anxiety, but they were now transferred to the Naval Barge "A.L. 3", after which "Fossa's" crew spent the rest of that night trying furiously to float her. Daylight revealed them still trying, when a destroyer arrived and ordered the Master to abandon ship. Having been taken off by a Belgian trawler, the crew called again at Dunkirk and on Monday morning were landed at Dover.

Is it not curious that human nature so rarely is affected by the obvious? We take with little thanks so much which is around us; accept with a minimum of gratitude those things which are essential for our very existence. As a nation we are fairly conscious of our debt to the Royal Navy, but how indifferently do we ever recognise all that is owed to the Merchant Navy for bringing home our food and raw materials! Past mines and the hidden menace of submarines, running the ambush of guns and bombs and machine-gun bullets, these lightly armed traders arrive from overseas defiant of the enemy's frightfulness.

In the last war only the introduction of food-cards and meatless days caused the average landsman to remember that our supplies travelled by danger-routes, and ever since then a certain newly-born respect for the Mercantile Service has been generally conceded. But, somehow, this belonged only to those deep-draught ocean carriers from some distant trade-route. It needed Dunkirk to remind the public how vast and detailed is our non-naval shipping, how large a commerce is done up and down the coast, across the Narrow Seas, in small tonnage driven by steam engines or motors.

No evacuated soldier will ever regard these little vessels except with the most profound gratitude. But what surprised everyone — not least the Navy and Army alike — was the extraordinary adaptability of peaceful seafarers suddenly called upon to endure war's severest tests.

Of this there could be no better example than afforded by the Motor Vessel "Seine" belonging to Rochester. Called from her regular avocation to Tilbury, she was demagnetised on May 28 whilst lying at the landing stage and considered immune from magnetic mines. Then she loaded 3500 cleansed petrol-tins full of drinking water for the troops, went up the Medway to Sheerness, where she took aboard another 1700 tins of water together with a naval officer and four naval ratings, and at 3 p.m. on May 30 arrived off Nieuport. Here the shore batteries immediately welcomed her with a hot fire, but she carried on further west down the coast and reached Bray, which lies between La Panne and Dunkirk. The "Seine's" people expected that the French soldiers coming off from Bray Dunes would be only too glad to carry for their comrades these tins of water, but such a request was not enthusiastically received.

"*Eau potable*?" they shrugged their shoulders. "*Ah! Mais non.*"

Well, that was all right for "Seine" if they didn't want this cargo, but what annoyed Captain C. V. Cogger, his Mate, Engineer, and two deckhands after all this trouble was that when the French soldiers eagerly leapt aboard, these *poilus* did not make fast the rowing-boat, which of course drifted off down the tide.

But where was the British Expeditionary Force? It was only later that the "Seine" learned our men were farther up the coast at La Panne, so thither the ship motored. Some British Army officers appeared, who were asked if they required the fresh water. And when the same negative reply was forthcoming, the "Seine" at once concentrated on evacuation.

By 7 p.m. she had loaded up to her limit — 352 French and British — so began the return voyage. And was it fierce? An armoured man-of-war might have winced a little, but this small motor coaster seemed destined to have less than the slenderest chance of survival when, abreast of Nieuport, the batteries blazed away vehemently. History indeed was repeating itself. Did not an earlier generation of German artillerymen, in the autumn of 1914, from this same Nieuport send their missiles whizzing against British destroyers and sloops?

Perhaps twenty-six years ago the enemy's gunners there were better trained? Or our warships less lucky than the Rochester cargo-carrier? At any rate, the remarkable sequel is that though sixteen shells all fell quite close to "Seine", not one ever touched her. Soldiers and sailors breathed freely once more, the motor ship held on her course for England, but those disappointed batteries must have called up their aircraft.

That night, whilst crossing the North Sea, "Seine" was subjected to another attack: this time from the Nazi Air Force. One bomb fell very near, twice she was machine-gunned, yet despite all this no casualties occurred. She managed to gain the North Goodwins, anchored there till daylight and by eight o'clock on Friday, May 31, was landing her 352 soldiers on Ramsgate quay. A very fine bit of valuable work.

But there was no rest for the "Seine". That same day she motored back to Dunkirk, and at 5 p.m. anchored with just enough cable to hold her against the tide. Ready for any emergency, she kept her engines running, and the wisdom of such a decision speedily showed itself. For at 5-30 p.m., in the words of her skipper, Captain C. V. Cogger, "Twenty enemy bombers appeared and performed."

The situation looked alarming until our warships' guns took up the challenge, one 'plane being brought down, others were driven off, but twenty minutes later these reappeared and again were dispersed.

This gave "Seine" opportunity to weigh anchor, keep on the move instead of remaining a steady target, and then she pluckily went close in to the shore — just long enough to get about 320 troops (mostly British) aboard. By 8 p.m. she was heading for the Kentish cliffs, and again expected to make her landfall near the North Goodwins lightship. The tide, however, carried her rather too far south and she struck the sands.

Luckily the sea happened to be smooth with no wind. Several times her bottom knocked the Goodwins, but with the rising tide floated off and at 9-30 a.m. her second lot of troops were marching down Ramsgate quay.

A little rest this time?

By no means. At noon she was under way for the same death-dealing Dunkirk, and by 8 p.m. underwent the usual bombing, which went on for more than an hour with terrific anger. Then she dashed in between the piers, lay alongside, embarked 300 more warriors, slipped ropes at 9-30 p.m., and was within Ramsgate by 7 a.m. on June 2. Her dead-beat crew had thus worked continuously during four days and nights without a spell of rest. But how great was the strain also on human nerves throughout nocturnal watching and avoiding the missiles which dropped from sky or were trajected from shore you may readily guess. June 3 seemed to the "Seine" something quite abnormal: an interval hardly comprehensible. It was summed up perfectly by the five words which Captain Cogger employed in concluding his report:

"Today we had some sleep."

Yes: these mariners worked themselves beyond all limits, and for some of them the effects were not quickly overcome. Nothing, however, could better illustrate our seafaring traditions than the heroic spirit which such men manifested throughout those terrible days.

Another small motor vessel, "Sequacity", owned by Messrs. F. T. Everard & Sons, was under the command of Captain J. Macdonald. She had been lying in the Downs several days when at four o'clock on the morning of Monday May 27 she received orders to proceed in company with the 823 tons S.S. "Yewdale". Before departure the "Sequacity" took aboard for self-protection one Bren gun, two soldiers, and a young naval rating named Evans, who brought with him Lewis guns, which the crew fixed up on the open bridge. It was Evans who, by maintaining bravely an incessant fire with these weapons and manfully sticking to his job, was to earn Captain Macdonald's high admiration.

All went well until abreast of Calais, when shells from the shore began flopping ahead, then nearer and nearer. Soon one penetrated the port side of the main hold at the waterline and went out through the starboard side. Sending the Mate down with some of the crew to patch up the holes, the Master tried to dodge the enemy's attentions, but the next shot entered the engine-room, smashed up the auxiliary machinery, put the switchboard out of action, and made it impossible for the pumps to continue ridding the hold of sea-water. Bad enough as the situation now seemed, it was made worse when a third shell entered the wheelhouse, passed down the fore hold, and right through the "Sequacity's" bottom.

The steamer was a little seaward of the motor vessel, but both now edged away from the shore, when suddenly eleven Nazi aeroplanes soared overhead and began bombing both ships. Whilst the naval rating did his best to keep the enemy off by incessant fire from his Lewis guns, one more shell from the shore burst over the motor vessel's fiddley, putting the Bren gun out of action, and wounding the Chief Engineer.

To increase the Master's anxiety, wind and an ugly choppy sea sprang up, which drove a lot of water through the apertures; and since the pumps could not function, a heavy list quickly developed.

"I blew my whistle for the steamer to stand by us", related the Master, "but she did not hear. A British 'plane then arrived, saw our trouble, flew ahead and dropped some red flares. The steamer then understood, turned round towards us, and we launched our boat. Our ship sank alongside the steamer, which, though badly peppered and bombed, managed to take us aboard and eventually land us at a southeast English port."

Still ignoring the dangers, back went the steamer across Channel to Dunkirk and here loaded up with 900 evacuated soldiers. Once more she headed for home, but en route the Nazi warplanes did their damnedest. Swooping low, they killed 7 weary soldiers, wounded 77, injured the Mate's leg seriously, and slightly hurt other members of the crew. The chart house had been ruined, navigating instruments destroyed, large holes thrust in the hull by shells. But this gallant band of men stuck to their job heroically, their Lewis gun even brought down one of the attacking planes, and the soldiers that survived were lucky to step ashore. But the Mate's leg had to be amputated.

Still undismayed by all that he had witnessed and experienced, the plucky Master, conscious that his steamer was pierced and so badly leaking that the authorities would not permit her to resume, at once got on to the telephone, rang up his owners and in the name of himself and his wonderful crew pleaded to be given another ship that they might go out for a further attempt.

And these were mercantile mariners untrained in the art and discipline of warfare.

It is this sudden change-over from peaceable livelihood to the midst of the most violent sort of warfare which made the Merchant Navy's work at once so magnificent and inspiriting. Suddenly for mariners to lay aside all they had been accustomed to learn in their daily lives, and readjust their perspective, demands more than simple effort. For the basic principle of service aboard ships of commerce is the very antithesis of fighting.

The primary duty, whether of passenger vessel or cargo carrier, is to avoid danger, preserve their owners' property in the best condition and bring the ship safely into port. Always at the back of these mariners is the possibility of ruining a fine reputation for caution and reliability: if a Master should not lose his 'ticket', he might by some chance or error of judgement forfeit at least the Company's approbation, and a fatal black mark then bring finish to an honourable career.

Therefore, this complete transformation of "Safety-First" ideals into "Risk-for-all-you're-worth", and at sudden bidding, came as a startling novelty. Sailors are often accused of being sentimental. That is because their daily avocation makes them intense realists. Navigating in thick weather, handling their vessels through heavy seas, nursing hull and machinery under anxious conditions, and finally winning through into port — these are the things which bind ship to mariner with a rare affection. The breaking of such a bond, the wreck of that hull which has meant more than home, is something very considerable and personal.

Thus we can begin to understand the bitter grief which Captains and crews experienced when a beloved vessel had to be left on Dunkirk beach, or below the pea-green waters of the North Sea. Almost it seemed as if a long and happy marriage had been snapped without the slightest warning.

To men of middle age, unaccustomed by habit to readapt their outlook, this meant a big and difficult shock. For the younger officers and men these new conditions created reactions that differed according to their characteristics. The ardent enthusiast longing for wild adventure, and finding modem seafaring altogether too humdrum, obviously discovered in Dunkirk the happiest chapter of his young life; and I know of one who brought back from that litter of death and spoil not merely romance but a free motor-bicycle. He had lived all the excitements which hitherto were found only in fiction, and a return to normal seafaring did not come too gladly.

But there was another young man, serving below decks in the engineering department of a steamer whose career at sea had barely begun. A good fellow, keen on his job, but sensitive by nature, frankly he did not relish all these bombing attacks what time his ship lay alongside Dunkirk pier. The thuds and explosions sounded even worse down there than outside in the open, and at last he could stand it no longer. Rushing on deck, his nerves utterly distraught, he felt that the trials could no longer be maintained.

There a wise and considerate deck-officer, understanding the youngster's feelings, and appreciating exactly the situation, suggested that this junior should try his hand at a Bren gun.

The idea was accepted — along flew a German bomber about to make further attack. The young man took aim, released a burst of fire and — believe it or not — down crashed bomber into the sea. This incident re-established the nervous man's morale, he went back to his job below and carried on with a new delight in living.

Some of these reports are remarkably laconic, but with a little imagination we can read between the lines and picture for ourselves what sailors went through. The following, reported by Lieut. R. Helyer, Chief Engineer of the "Royal Eagle" concerning this vessel's share in the evacuation, is just plain, bald, matter of fact. But at the back of this statement how much tragedy belongs!

"Left early May 29th and arrived La Panne about 9 a.m. Ship's A.A. Guns in action all day, heavy bombing during the day but not hit. Left at dusk and arrived at Margate Pier at Daylight 30th May. Landed between 800-900 troops.

"Left Margate 30th and arrived about 1 p.m. Before arriving La Panne shelled by shore Gun Batteries from upper end of beach, but no damage. Again ship's A.A. guns in Action. Bombed during day but not hit. Left at Dusk and arrived 7.30 a.m. 31st May Sheerness. Machine gunned at night coming back by Plane but think it was only guide for M.T. Boat as French Destroyer 3 miles astern went up.

"All troops were taken from beach, and landed: between 1800 to 1900, about 40 wounded. Oil, watered and cleaned up ship. Proceeded to Ramsgate left on 1st June for Dunkirk, arrived at dusk waited off shore all night. Shelling heavy all night and a few dents in ship but no one hurt.

"French drifter brought off mostly French troops. Last hour three boat loads of wounded arrived some very bad cases. Left at daylight and arrived Sheerness 6 p.m. 3rd June but were recalled at 8 p.m. as Evacuation was finished."

The "Queen of Thanet", which was stationed at Granton in the Firth-of-Forth as Flotilla Leader of Minesweepers, received instructions on Thursday, during the evacuation, to proceed to Dunkirk. On arrival there, this vessel with many others proceeded to take in troops off the beach under terrific bombing and shell-fire from the Germans; in spite of this she received several hundreds of troops and proceeded to Margate Jetty where they were disembarked. Arrangements were then made for her to take in oil fuel and proceed again to Dunkirk, as soon as possible; she arrived over the following evening, took on board several hundred more troops and many wounded, and again proceeded to Margate Jetty, disembarked the troops, and after taking in stores and water proceeded for Dunkirk. When more than halfway across the Channel they noticed a steamer, now in difficulties and seriously damaged, which had been bombed and was loaded with 3,000 troops; on arriving close to the vessel she proved to be the London North Eastern Mail Steamer, "Prague."

A destroyer was alongside transferring troops numbering 500 from the disabled vessel. A wireless message was then received by the "Queen of Thanet" asking her to call alongside also, and take off the troops. When within hailing distance, the Commanding Officer of the "Queen of Thanet", Lieutenant Commander Hallivell, R.N.V.R., asked: "How many troops are left on board", and the reply came: "2000." Commander

Hallivell replied: "I will take the lot". These were all safely embarked, including the few wounded, and again the vessel left for Margate Jetty; this on Sunday.

In the meantime the "Prague" having been lightened was able with precaution to proceed under her own steam to Dover on Sunday night. "Queen of Thanet" again proceeded to Dunkirk, and early Monday morning cleaned up the beach and brought over a few troops, including 47 wounded. The total number of troops brought over by the "Queen of Thanet" was 4,000 plus wounded. Lieutenant Commander Hallivell has since been promoted Commander.

CHAPTER VIII — ALONG THE BEACHES

JUST as some people always seem to get mixed up in adventure, so with certain places. Dunkirk throughout the centuries has managed to obtain more than its share of wars. Five and a half centuries ago it was burnt by the English, later on the Spaniards took it, next it became French, then after the Battle of the Dunes our country were the owners till Charles II sold it back to France. Most of the people still spoke Flemish when in the First Great War it was a great Anglo-French naval base and Germans nightly began dropping their bombs.

So nobody could well be surprised that, in this Second Great War, Dunkirk should find itself amidst the old environment of flames and fierce fighting; or that those tufted ridges of dunes, from which its name derives, should once more have become history's backcloth.

If you want a mental picture, consider Dunkirk as having a back and front. In the former was a rather drab but busy seaport — all docks and basins, cranes and canals, cargo steamers coming in and out and blowing their syrens with that shrill note peculiar to the French.

But, along the front, the yellow sands dry out to the extent of half and even three-quarters of a mile at lowest tides, all the way from Calais, past Gravelines, even into Belgium and Holland. Our immediate attention, however, is concerned with that nine-mile stretch from Dunkirk past Malo-les-Bains casino to the spot called La Panne. Within this area the drama of death had made a platform for itself.

When the decision was made to withdraw the B.E.F. from France, Dunkirk alone remained practicable. Yet because its docks and warehouses already had been made the chief targets for aerial bombs, oil dumps set ablaze, buildings gutted by fire, roads hollowed out into craters, only two embarkation methods availed. Either by sending small open boats on to the beach as ferries between the dunes and ships anchored off in deep water, or else by taking vessels just inside the two jetties which define the harbour's entrance channel long before shipyard and dockland commence.

But the difficulties were manifold. A strong tide sluices past the beach, making rowing a hard task. Moreover the jetties had never been built for embarkation: they were just breakwaters through whose piles the pea-soup current surges and batters itself. At Low Water there is not so much as even fifteen feet and only in the middle, but you will appreciate that with a width of less than 150 yards little enough space remained for either 1200-tons destroyer or broad-beamed paddle steamer to come alongside, let alone emerge stern-first in the darkness, with all lights out, and bombs and shells crashing universally.

Let it equally be appreciated that whilst only a few vessels within this narrow approach could lie alongside at a time, neither guns nor tanks, neither lorries nor stores of any kind, could be taken aboard. Just the men and their rifles, and nothing else. This harbour-entrance is exposed to northerly winds, which drive a boisterous swell between the piles and a dangerous surf on to the beaches.

But the greatest fear persisted all the while that collision, or some other accident, might sink a ship athwart this defile and block it up. That such a disaster did not completely cork up the opening, till after evacuation, was but one item in the miracle of Dunkirk. Seamanship, cool handling of vessels in a tight corner, eyes glancing everywhere, had much to do with the triumph.

Yet much more than that was required of the mariner.

Curiously contrasted was the effect of this bombing alike on some ships and some people. One typical British collier during her second visit to Dunkirk was there shelled by either a shore battery or a perambulating tank. The first shot killed two of her crew on deck, injuring another who died the next day, and it also jammed the steering gear. A second projectile burst in the Master's cabin, destroyed his medicine chest, and carried away part of the bridge. A third shell exploded in the engine-room, bringing death to both engineers, whilst still more shells made jagged holes in the ship's sides.

Yet, notwithstanding all this slaughter and damage, the crew fixed up the steering gear, made some repairs, and brought their vessel under her own power safely into Dover.

Then there was a small British cargo-carrier of 1000 tons returning with German prisoners in the hold and a number of British army officers on deck. Suddenly alongside dashed one of the enemy's fast motor-torpedo boats, who demanded surrender. The reply came without delay when British officers and men blazed away with their "Tommy" guns so determinedly that the enemy was left disabled; but when this news had been conveyed to one of the German officer prisoners, the latter made one exclamation: "Thank God!", he remarked.

All this sort of work, with opportunity neither for meals nor rest, continuous hours of duty under heavy fire, always on the alert and death awaiting them every moment of the day and night, tried human nerves and bodies beyond all physical endurance. Soldiers who had been on the march for days, swimming canals, then hiding like rabbits in the dunes, were not more worn out than the sailors who kept braving the hazards to bring succour.

The first large bodies of the B.E.F. began reaching Dunkirk on Sunday, May 26. Monday started its bombardment at 8-30 a.m. and rarely eased up. In the cellars of ruined houses, or lying along the sands, tired troops suffered the raids until soon after 6 p.m. their weary eyes beheld with joy several destroyers, a hospital ship, half a dozen trawlers arriving. After sunset, whilst oil tanks in the docks shot sheets of flames into the sky, and ammunition dumps persistently exploded, men filed down in orderly fashion to the jetties, and the beaches from Dunkirk to Malo were lit up by the glare of burning buildings.

That night some 5000 of these soldiers congregated along the dunes, half choked by the dense smoke. Small boats grated their keels into the sand, stretcher cases and walking wounded were fetched to the water's edge and ferried away. An army officer would inquire of the boatman, "How many?"

"Room for eight." And oars would soon be pulling across the tide.

Then more boats would fill up, men wade out to meet the rest, whilst troops from hiding holes took their places in the long unending trail. From overhead Nazi 'planes were dropping magnesium flares; many a foot-sore hungry soldier fell mortally struck by bullets, yet the thin dark line silhouetted against the flames pressed slowly on, hoping to be taken afloat ere another sunrise should concentrate worse dangers.

Suspense is too slight a word to describe the patient suffering as these men's lives were poised between death and life. Here was not a rabble running away, but a whole army defying all hazards and taking to the sea according to schedule and orderly plan.

Often enough their fathers had told them of the retreat from Mons, their uncles had waxed eloquent concerning the Gallipoli withdrawal. But these, their successors, had been fighting and marching over 75 miles in the last three days, some had travelled 30 miles daily for most of a week, others had been contending 17 days and nights without respite.

Now, however, it was to be the Navy's privilege to waft them across the water. And — solely because we possessed command of the sea — this responsibility could be carried out with confidence.

Many of the incredible adventures of our sailors, soldiers and airmen will never be related, just as a complete record of all rescuing fleet is out of the question. We know only in part, and the remainder met death without even the names of their ships being recorded. Most of the great gallantries occurred in the dark hours between 11 p.m. and 3-30 a.m., whilst embarkation was taking place under cover of night, yet some of these noble deeds could not escape notice.

Take, for instance, the ceaseless toil of Major Gilbert Sydney Jones, of the Lincolns. Forgetful of long marches, he spent the night of June 1-2 standing up to his chest in the Dunkirk sea, assisting his men into the boats. Everybody was tired and tottering, shells were falling around, men bearing the weight of arms and sodden clothing could hardly energise their bodies through the water. But for this officer they would certainly have been drowned.

The anxious night dragged on, steamers arrived in the roadstead, filled up and hurried away. Boatload after boatload left the beach, but with the coming of dawn it was impossible to expose the men as enemy raiders swept down the sky. So, almost on the point of collapse, he hurried the remainder of his soldiers to a corner of the beach where they dug themselves in and waited for another night after a long day's assaults, and finally he was able to get them afloat from death's embrace. Major Jones well deserved the D.S.O. with which he was now awarded.

I remember that a French *poilu*, fresh from Dunkirk, told me that the Allies' weakness there was lack of aeroplanes.

"*Pas d'avions!*" he insisted somewhat inaccurately.

Actually the close co-operation of our Naval and Coastal Command aircraft maintained unceasing patrols to assist the evacuation. Without such vigilance the transport route between England and France would have been as dangerous as that wet corridor which lies between the

Flemish banks and Dunkirk's dunes. So many enemy 'planes were thus shot down in vigorous combat, so many others badly damaged and forced to seek escape only by jettisoning their bombs, that hundreds of ships, and thousands of lives, were able to pass in security. For the most part we kept the enemy's flyers between Calais and Dunkirk, where the sky had been turned into one long battle scene.

As one of our pilots expressed it, the atmosphere was so thick with every sort of machine that they reminded him of midges at the end of a summer's day. When on Thursday, May 30, a dense fog intervened — to the enemy's great annoyance — this kindly curtain covering ships and beaches temporarily caused a marked decrease in aerial activity. But for the best part of two days a northwesterly wind turned this lee-shore into an impossible stretch of white-topped waves.

For a while the situation looked serious, precious moments were ticking by, the German Army's pressure was increasing rapidly, soon it would be irresistible. Thousands and thousands of our men had still to be sent afloat ere those in the rear could be dealt with. The threat of annihilation seemed real, occasionally everything appeared to go wrong, powerful destroyers crumpled up and sank like cardboard models, boats capsized their human freights, lifebelts were seen floating empty down the tide, ambulances coming into the town were blown to bits before reaching the water.

It all suggested the saddest chapter in civilisation's story.

But that was only the external shape of things. For never could the standard of British morale have been higher, never did torn uniforms disguise such fighting ardour.

A good sleep. A long drink. A square meal.

Then these men with bandaged arms and battered helmets would be ready to finish a job which fate and treachery had interrupted.

CHAPTER IX — THE BARGE FLEET GOES TO WAR

THE auxiliary barge "Pudge" was lying outside Millwall Dock on May 29, when she was requisitioned and towed down to Tilbury, where three days' rations were put aboard ready for the great adventure.

After the tug "Ocean Cock" brought her next day, together with the barges "Doris", "Ena" and "Tollesbury", into Dover, they lay alongside the Prince of Wales Pier. At 8-30 a.m., on May 31, all barge captains were summoned ashore and addressed by a naval officer.

"Volunteers," he told them, "are wanted for Dunkirk. Nobody will be compelled, but we shall be very grateful if you will offer your services."

At that moment altogether 17 of these barges had reached Dover Harbour, and every one of the gallant Captains instantly showed a readiness to take his ship across to Dunkirk. Readers whose knowledge of such vessels has been derived chiefly from the popular short stories of W. W. Jacobs, or from some casual glimpse of a black hull dropping down on the tide through the London bridges with masts lowered, may be reminded that the Thames barge traces her ancestry back through seventeenth-century Dutch vessels with rare pride and dignity. Her rig, except for slight modifications, has continued with the most amazing conservatism from generation to generation, and her picturesque chocolate sails are part of the Lower Thames' background.

But let there be no mistake about these highly specialised craft. They demand a very particular sort of seamanship, to which most sailormen are completely unsuited. Watch the barge Captain, and his crew of one, sailing with a hot tide past Woolwich, or threading a course among the busy waters just below the Pool of London among cargo steamers and tugs; you need little convincing that the job is such as belongs exclusively to a veritable artist.

To almost any other seafarer this difficult handling would appear worse than a thousand nightmares. The whole secret of success lies in years of experience — knowledge of the east coast tides and shoals, familiarity with Thames and Medway, intimate acquaintance with Essex creeks and such harbours as Ramsgate or Dover. Apart from occasional visits to Rye and Newhaven, the barge normally does not trade to the westward.

A considerable amount of cargo is carried between the London river and the northern ports up to Harwich and Ipswich. These craft are unrivalled for floating into a mere gully, shifting berth under no more spread of canvas than their topsail, and settling themselves comfortably on the ground where most vessels would soon come to a bad end.

But precisely these unusual qualities were to make our London barges so desirable when the cry from Dunkirk beaches was heard across the English Channel. Yet how strange it sounded! Certainly sea-warfare creates curious surprises. In the last period of hostilities against Germany the world heard with amazement of tramp steamers and schooners, having hidden guns, going forth as "Q-ships" to fight U-boats. More than two decades passed by, and now in this second war the Navy actually requested the services of sailing barges! Incredible! And still more amazing in this the most mechanised of all ages!

It was at once decided to select from the seventeen that had assembled within Dover's breakwaters the following three sailing barges which possessed auxiliary motors: "Pudge", "Lady Rosebery", and "Thyra". But also were quickly chosen the "Doris", "Duchess", and "H.A.C.", these three having no other power than their sails.

Throughout the Dunkirk days nothing was more significant than the joy of a chosen ship, and the bitter grief when some volunteer had to be 'turned down One firm of owners told me how a good little vessel had been first accepted, but finally rejected, because at the last minute the authorities were compelled to change the plans. The ship's Master took the matter to heart and suffered such bitter disappointment that he almost broke down and wept. The Dunkirk drama thus came and went without this brave mariner's share in it.

A few weeks later, whilst still pursuing his trading voyages, ship and crew fell on the hardest fate of all. Precisely what happened we may never know. The ship became overdue, and nothing but her empty boat was ever found. An aerial bomb? A U-boat's torpedo? Yes, either of these would have sufficed. But Dunkirk, with all its horrors, could have brought to that ship's crew a wonderful happiness.

Thus when the big tug "St. Fabian", on May 31, took in tow the three barges "Pudge", "Doris" and "Lady Rosebery" at the end of a powerful

7-inch wire and began heading towards Dunkirk, all hands congratulated themselves on their good fortune. Crews had been clearly instructed as to what would be required of them, that after tugs had brought the tows to some spot between one and eight miles east of Dunkirk, the men were to use their own initiative and get their barges on to the beach in as shallow water as possible. All assistance must then be rendered in enabling troops to wade or walk aboard.

In like manner, that same day, the "Thyra" and "H.A.C." were towed across by the tug "St. Abbs", though the "Duchess" broke adrift and was picked up by a naval vessel which brought her safely over to the French coast.

Never had the English Channel seen such a strange procession, nor did a barge fleet ever experience such thrilling adventures. That series of events began quite early when the "Centaur" of Colchester, after being towed to Dover, broke away from her tug and drove on to the pier, damaging it and herself. This reduced the number to sixteen.

Every sailor will appreciate the inevitable problem of towing ships that have been generally accustomed to proceed under their own power. Even on the calmest day, Dover's Straits are subject to a swell which puts a severe strain on ropes and gear. The low freeboard of a barge, her behaviour in a seaway, the sudden jerk which comes as she rises to a wave or falls in a trough — these items could not now be considered very carefully. Time sufficed merely to get these flat-bottomed hulls across to La Panne or Dunkirk with the least possible delay. Weary warriors, just escaped from death time after time, awaited the arrival of the only ship-type that could safely place herself ashore, fill up with a living cargo, and then float off with the flood tide.

Expeditious progress from Dover therefore was the first consideration, and the barges must be hurried towards Dunkirk despite all the snapping of ropes. In addition to those already named went the "Glenway" and "Lark", the "Spurgeon" from Leigh-on-Sea, the "Ethel Everard" and "Royalty" of Greenhithe, the "Tollesbury", "Beatrice Maud", "Barbara Jean", "Ena" and the "Aidie". Others were indeed requisitioned, but not taken up, and it is illustrative of the difficult trials to be endured that, of the sixteen which actually reached Dunkirk's inferno, only eight ever returned. The rest either were sunk by enemy action or had to be abandoned.

Now to a stranger — in war time, with most lights out, position of buoys uncertain, and a quite strong tide — the approach towards Dunkirk Roads is by no means easy. Apart from the many shoals, the not less dangerous minefields had to be remembered. The tug "St. Fabian" found great difficulty in locating the inshore channel, as her captain possessed neither local knowledge nor chart. However, by daybreak (Saturday, June 1) she brought "Pudge", "Doris" and "Lady Rosebery" to a position some three miles east of the Dunkirk entrance, where the half light revealed the black spots on the brown sands to be not flies but thousands of soldiers. And shouts proved they were still alive.

High water would be about 8-30 a.m., so with the rising tide a barge could gradually work her way well up the beach this morning. Having consulted with a destroyer, the "St. Fabian's" captain now ordered "Lady Rosebery" to start up her auxiliary motor, pick up the "Doris", and both to get well inshore for the waiting troops.

Scarcely were these instructions being carried out, with the "Pudge" too starting up her engine, than Captain W. Watson of the latter with his Mate, A. Hall, felt a terrific explosion. And when they glanced across the water there was no longer any tug. She had been blown to destruction. Possibly by a mine.

Captain Watson lost no time in lowering "Pudge's" small boat, rowed about in the semi-darkness, and discovered one man. This man, a stoker, had been on watch in the tug's stokehold when suddenly the force blew him out through a hole into the sea. And now he was suffering from a broken leg.

Whilst he was being hauled into the boat, a second man (the tug's Mate) also clambered in, and these two were the "St. Fabian's" sole survivors. Then, relates Captain Watson, "I saw another small boat approaching and hailed them, to find they were the crews of 'Doris' and 'Lady Rosebery' which had been sunk in the explosion. They had scrambled aboard their boat before their barges sank. All happened so quickly, that it is difficult to remember everything, but my barge seemed to be lifted bodily out of the water."

It was a startling enough occurrence, at the end of her first voyage, for "Pudge" to find herself alone. Leaking badly because of the concussion, she could certainly do little good if she remained. Along came a destroyer, who therefore ordered her to carry on back to England with the injured survivors, and this she proceeded to do. Luckily after five miles another large tug overtook her and brought her into Ramsgate, where she arrived before midday.

The glorious First of June! How curiously had British Naval history been associated with this date! Twenty-four short years ago the Battle of Jutland was nearing its end. Today the desperate Dunkirk episode had not yet reached its climax. It was 5 a.m. by the time "St. Abbs" arrived with "Thyra" and "H.A.C.", and cast off. Thereupon "Thyra" towed "H.A.C." on to the beach, where "we got eleven French soldiers off to our barge", said Captain E. W. Filley of the former. "Other groups of soldiers refused to come, as they wanted to reach France and not England."

The advent of day heralded a fierce bombing, and the barge men without steel helmets or any sort of protection now were in the thick of considerable liveliness. Gradually they worked their hulls with the tide up the sandy beach, where they found the "Glenway" and "Lark", which had come across laden with stores, the idea being that the French would obtain these after the tide ebbed. But so viciously developed the enemy's attack that from both of these vessels the crews were ordered out, together with eight British soldiers then aboard.

"Thyra" rescued the lot, including those from "H.A.C.", but it was a terribly trying experience. During nine thrilling hours Captain Filley expected every minute to be the last. He had been plunged into the war with all its intensity and horror that seemed so contrasted with Medway sailing. Whilst his "Thyra" lay on, or near, the shore from 5 a.m. to 2 p.m. she seemed to be the selected target for Nazi aeroplanes' bombs and machine-gun fire. True, there developed a lull about noon, when ten of our R.A.F. fighters came over, drove about thirty German bombers away, shooting four of them down; but otherwise it was just one long suspense.

It may sound ridiculous and incredible, but "Thyra" was never hit. Yet had she stayed there much longer, quite obviously all the twenty-eight men aboard would be lost with the ship. The tugs having disappeared, Captain Filley decided it was his duty to get away with these survivors.

But what a return voyage! The enemy aloft still persisted in an endeavour to sink everything which floated, regardless of size or species. Whilst still not far from the French coast and in company with a trawler, five bombs fell from the sky. Again it looked as if nothing could prevent destruction, but actually the missiles fell very closely between the two ships, though with such explosive force that "Thyra" was lifted quite a foot higher out of the water.

At last, when half-way towards England, the tug "Empire Henchman" hove in sight, took her in tow and brought her into Dover just before midnight. Grazed, splintered, her engine damaged, bollards badly strained through much towing, the "Thyra" was lucky to have come through as well as she did. But hear the experiences of the sailing barge "Duchess", which we saw arriving off Dunkirk after breaking adrift on passage.

This Saturday, June 1, will never be forgotten by barge crews of the southeast coast: it will always remain the biggest day since London River's craft witnessed the Great Fire of London. At 2-30 a.m., that is to say about dead low water, the "Duchess" beached herself and, as day broke, the troops began boarding until no fewer than ninety soldiers had been received.

With daylight and half flood about 5 a.m. came a light breeze, which enabled "Duchess" to float off the sand and get away bound for England. You can picture for yourself the unusual sight of all this khaki-clad crowd against the red-ochred canvas. To any seafaring man it looked the oddest combination imaginable. It is doubtful if one of those warriors till now had previously stepped aboard a sailing vessel, but which of them could have expected to be transported in this fashion?

As if to complicate matters, the barge barely had cleared the land than wind died away and left her rolling in a flat calm. The heavy sprit which makes a diagonal across the mainsail swayed to and fro, blocks creaked, ropes slatted idly. Ninety soldiers in their unprecedented environment wondered what would happen next. They had battled with German Armies, been swimming French canals, experienced the onslaughts alike of aeroplanes and tanks. But this *mal de mer* in a Channel swell was worse than all their troubles so far.

Then another ship showed up. A sharp-bowed vessel in a hurry, cleaving her way through the oily calm towards the "Duchess".

"That's a destroyer!"

Easing engines, she came alongside the wooden vessel, and a naval commanding officer called from the high bridge to Captain H. Wildish at the barge's wheel. "I'll relieve you of the soldiers," said the former. "Go back to the beach and fetch some more."

Thus to one already lengthy chapter of incidents these tired troops now added the novel experience of being transferred at sea from sail to steam. But they had originally reached "Duchess" much more than merely fatigued and foot-sore. Thirsty and hungry, gladly they had accepted the drinking water and limited rations that had been intended for only two men, so now the barge was bereft of all supplies. This the destroyer quickly remedied by passing down ample provisions, after which the two ships parted and set off in opposite directions. The soldiers now were feeling happier with such a fast warship beneath their feet. The white cliffs of England would soon await them.

But behold the chances and changes of human life! The uncertainties of ships and men!

The emptied "Duchess" set a course again for the perilous beach, a little breeze sprang up and enabled Captain Wildish to trim his sails. Tonight he would again be in the hottest corner of Europe, but the destroyer …

Those Nazi aviators must have witnessed the transference, and noticed the khaki ranks; for out flew the war 'planes, swooped low over the destroyer, bombed her heavily and without mercy, so that when last seen the British man-of-war was in a sinking condition. How soon would it be the turn of "Duchess"?

On reaching the sand, she found herself between Dunkirk and La Panne with three other barges as neighbours: "Aidie", "Ethel Everard", and "Royalty". These had come across laden with ammunition, but so intolerable was the violent bombing by enemy 'planes that the first two had been abandoned as they lay. Wildish had a hurried consultation with "Royalty's" skipper and it was decided that as there apparently were no soldiers left on the beach by now, the only thing was to abandon both "Duchess" and "Royalty",

For a while they hesitated, when a motorboat passed near.

"Could you give us a tow off?"

But the motorboat replied that his engine was incapable.

So about 8 a.m. no alternative remained. The two barges were deserted and blown up, the crews taking to the "Duchess's" rowing boat which presently was picked up by the tug "Cervia".

Be it remembered that this week was the first time in history that a sailing craft with soldiers aboard was bombed from the air, as also the first occasion since the Anglo-Dutch wars that vessels of such a spritsail rig had taken active part in hostilities. Equally it may be surmised that such an occasion will not recur. The special occasion, combined with the geographical situation, provided these barges with a unique opportunity.

It will, therefore, be permissible and justifiable if we further add to these details from collateral accounts, before memories become dimmed or personal records perish. Who can say that, with the rapid advance of the internal combustion motor towards universality, the purely sailing barge will not soon depart from the sea as surely as full-rigged ships have forsaken the ocean?

Dunkirk was really the culmination of the barges' war activities. Unobtrusively, they had like other small coasters, both in the last war and this, been carrying valuable essential stores from England to France. When the "Ethel Everard" set out from Dover on the afternoon of Friday, May 31, she carried a dangerous cargo of shells and small arms ammunition. Her tug simultaneously towed also the sailing barge "Tollesbury".

By 11-30 that night they were off Gravelines, and from then onwards it was just one long nerve-trying period of being machine-gunned or bombed. Nearly all these barges were in the act of beaching themselves soon after 1 a.m. that Saturday morning before Low Water, and "Ethel Everard", after slipping from the tug when about a mile east of Dunkirk piers, proceeded under sail till she took the ground. The manoeuvre was complicated not merely by reason of the aerial attacks, but because the playful swell knocked the barge's stern round so that she lay broadside on.

She had brought with her a sergeant and five soldiers who, perceiving some troops on the shore, hailed them, thinking that these must be the working party come to discharge the warlike stores. On the contrary, they were part of the foot-slogging thousands hoping to be evacuated.

Without delay these began climbing aboard, and their first request was as notable as urgent.

"Where d'you keep the drinking water, Skipper?"

The supply vanished not less quickly than had been the case aboard "Duchess", but a naval cutter from a near-lying gunboat fetched these

81

hungry men off and fed them. Then less than an hour later, as the bombing grew worse, the gunboat sent a boat to collect the crews of every barge on this untenable beach.

"You'll have to abandon them", a naval officer now told them. "We're going to set your craft on fire."

The decision had barely been made known than the warship's anti-aircraft guns pointing upwards to the sky loosed off three shells, and two 'planes fell down like a couple of dead birds. Every minute seemed to bring its own fresh excitement, since as the gunboat moved off inside Dunkirk breakwaters, four more aircraft zoomed over, the guns barked once more, and four 'planes fluttered helplessly to destruction. This provided a respite long enough for the ship to load up her full complement of troops and set out on her way to England.

Brave and resourceful as were these barge crews, cleverly as they brought their vessels to rest on the sands, there was little enough chance for defying the murderous menace from the sky with no sort of bullet-proof shelter. The sailing barge "Royalty" had arrived off Dunkirk about 8 a.m. that Saturday loaded with ammunition, stores, but also clean petrol-cans filled with drinking water for the troops. Six soldiers, as before, had been sent with her for supervising the cargo's discharge. When two miles east from the harbour, "Royalty" was made ready for beaching, cast off by the tug, and the enemy chose this as his selected moment.

"We were setting up our topsail", relates Captain H. Miller, her Master, "to carry out this operation, when a large number of German 'planes appeared overhead and immediately started bombing and machine-gunning us. When we arrived on the beach, we let go the anchor still being attacked, our decks continually sprayed with bullets."

Since no one came along to unload the stores, "Royalty" let down her boat in which the crew and six soldiers rowed off to the tug "Cervia". Abandonment having again become inevitable, at least it was comforting to claim this small steamer for temporary home. But as they advanced, they were hailed by a launch carrying twenty-five soldiers and sailors. The motor had broken down, so these passengers too were fortunate in their rescue. Still proceeding parallel with the land, the tug and its increasing party now came across the sailing barge "Tollesbury", whose Captain was standing on deck. But his adventures had already mounted rapidly. Her crew had begun by rowing this barge with sweeps on to the sands and taken off 200 soldiers. They then pushed her afloat with what a bargeman calls "setting booms", spread their sails, and got under way.

Now against the head wind and almost 3-knot tide, the "Tollesbury" could make no headway, try as she did, so she let go anchor. Luckily a destroyer realised her plight, dashed alongside and took the soldiers off. Thereupon "a terrible air raid" ensued, so the destroyer with her passengers had to clear off.

Two more destroyers gallantly approached to screen the barge, and both warships were sunk; yet though bombs were dropping all round the barge, "Tollesbury" was not hit. At this stage the above-mentioned tug arrived and passed a wire on board. Not surprisingly amid so much excitement and death-dealing missiles, the first aim was to get going quickly, but the tug started off at too great a pace so that she ripped the "Tollesbury's" windlass clean out of the deck. However, another wire was made fast, and the incident concluded with the safe arrival in England of the people from barges and the launch, together with the "Tollesbury" that had so narrowly escaped disaster. Troops having been landed, "Cervia" towed "Tollesbury" round to Gravesend.

It had been quite an exciting week-end, involving the losses of "Duchess", "Lady Rosebery", "Lark", "Ethel Everard", "Royalty", "Doris", "Barbara Jean" and "Aidie". Both "Glenway" and "Beatrice Maud", after assisting in the evacuation, got back home but had to be taken in hand for repairs. The "Ena" underwent the experience of being abandoned near Dunkirk but later, despite her damage, arrived off Deal and was sent to Ipswich to be repaired.

CHAPTER X — THE PLEASURE FLEET IN PERIL

WHEN we speak of a nation's sea-power we mean not merely her battleships and cruisers, her aircraft and destroyers, her submarines, and fast motor craft which skim the surface.

Primarily we reckon that vast collection of men and ships which belong to the carrying trade and fishing fleets; for, historically, it is from these that the fighting navies have always been obtained and maintained. Until comparatively recent years, that is to say long after the introduction of steam, the average citizen never went to sea except in pursuit of duty. Voyaging was such a solemn, serious, undertaking that a passenger bound across the ocean to India or America first sat down and made his will.

Then, gradually through the Victorian era with the improvements of marine shipbuilding and engineering, steamers became bigger, faster, safer, and with such improved accommodation that the old awe towards the sea departed and people actually chose to travel afloat for sheer choice. The science and art of navigation having developed so wonderfully, overseas trade having likewise extended to every corner of the globe, a fresh encouragement was given to what we now call 'liners'. The growth of prosperity first in the United States and then in Canada, the increase of commerce through the Suez Canal to India, Australia, and New Zealand, and the abolition of sailing vessels for comfortable and even luxurious steamships finally ended the old prejudice.

Thus each year witnessed the amassing of a huge mercantile fleet, always being kept up to date and replaced by newer tonnage, but ever ready for the country's service at a time of great crisis. In the Boer War such units were employed as transports, but when in August 1914 the First German War broke out it soon became possible to arm so many first-class passenger ships and turn them into merchant cruisers that they formed a navy within a navy.

In other words, sea-power had with little effort been suddenly extended in the most advantageous possible manner. So likewise that fine collection of steam trawlers accustomed in peace-time to go fishing off

Iceland and elsewhere was a fleet-in-being prepared to act as minesweepers, patrols, escorts, or whatever the country might require.

Nor did this immense reserve of ships and seafarers end at that. Whilst all sorts of steamers were needed for transporting soldiers and munitions, smaller carriers must keep the Royal Navy supplied with fuel and stores; for the mere feeding of so many thousand sailors afloat is an enormous business that would cause the heaviest strain unless we possessed a considerable number of moderate and small-sized vessels.

But during the last three generations our seafaring spirit has shown itself in a democratic manner never suspected by our forefathers. Busy citizens shackled to work-a-day routine began to find in coastal voyaging of day trips that very recreation and solace which modem conditions demanded. Yachting as a leading sport during the last fifty years, and especially in the last two decades, has produced not merely thousands of keen and competent amateurs, but sustained shipbuilding yards which at shortest notice could switch over their organisation for Admiralty work. Simultaneously all round the coast splendidly equipped excursion steamers and motor ships, of high power and remarkable deck space, were being given every encouragement by the newly enthusiastic public no longer reluctant to trust themselves on the sea.

So it came about that when this Second German War began in September 1939 British sea-power was something far mightier than any mid-Victorian might have contemplated. Our nautical strength, both as to ships and men, had been magnified beyond all imagining. If yachts could be assigned such duties as anti-submarine hunting, those popular pleasure paddlers which summer by summer gave health and rest to city dwellers could be employed troop-carrying, mine-sweeping, and so on.

But it was for the Dunkirk purpose that these excursion ships were so exactly suitable that they might have been built to no other purpose. Consider the problem which confronted. Ability to go alongside piers, maximum deck space for accommodating crowds, moderate draught, and a good turn of speed.

It was not a case of withdrawing troops from some distant theatre, but from across the North Sea's southern shores; therefore not cabined ships, but ample room on deck, aboard those vessels which could make a quick turn-round and keep on repeating the achievement, became the essential requirement.

Ludicrous that a paddler designed, built, and patronised for pleasure should find the climax of her existence in war! Strange that those wooden decks so familiar to holidaymakers of the Thames, South Coast, Bristol Channel, Medway, Clyde and elsewhere, should be trodden by khaki soldiers! Who ever expected that the steamers which took day-trippers from Brighton pier would come under enemy fire and be sunk? Who could imagine that Isle of Man packets, usually the very expression of holiday happiness, should take part in naval operations? Or that Llandudno should be associated with Dunkirk gallantry?

The obvious lesson is this: Great Britain being an island, entirely dependent on its nautical strength, must always go on developing and encouraging *every* branch of its seafaring ability. We cannot afford to neglect any one item, however small and trivial that might seem. The fundamental love of the sea in all its aspects must be kept ardent. If the Germans are inspired by the "Strength Through Joy" attitude, it is our national duty to ensure that people are given every opportunity for going afloat and perceiving the wonders of travel.

Our ship yards must never again be allowed to suffer neglect, our Mercantile Mariners never again permitted to 'chuck' their service and wander about looking for shore jobs because their ships have been laid up. Sea-minded! That disposition will have to be given a new animation, the carrying trade supported, crews allowed a more permanent security of tenure, the attractions of ocean adventure presented to our youth with greater directness.

And if Governmental subsidies should be found necessary, how better could public funds be expended? For the whole of our past history and future existence rest on the foundation of seafaring. Dunkirk in those few bitter days focused this fact with brilliant clarity.

Space will not enable us to discuss every exploit of all those gallant pleasure flotillas which did the right things at the right time and helped to rescue our B.E.F. from what threatened to be annihilation. We shall best serve our purpose if we offer characteristic incidents of accomplishment as in another chapter we have watched the work of the barges.

More than 170 of these 'minor' vessels were able to take part, and over ten per cent paid the death penalty. It is no longer a secret that the losses included such a miscellany as the steam yacht "Grive" (better known as "Narcissus"); the paddlers "Brighton Belle", "Brighton Queen", "Gracie

Fields", "Waverley", "Medway Queen", and "Crested Eagle"; the trawlers "Polly Johnston", "Thomas Bartlett", "Thuringia", "Calvi", "Stella Dorado", "Argyllshire", "Blackburn Rovers", "Westella"; the three drifters "Girl Pamela", "Paxton", "Boy Roy"; the two Armed Boarding Steamers "King Orry" and "Mona's Queen"; the dan-laying vessel "Comfort", and the tug "St. Fagan".

Some companies surrendered the greater part of their fleet for Admiralty service in general, or the Dunkirk duties in particular. For instance both of the above Armed Boarding Steamers belonged to the Isle of Man Steam Packet Co., but six other vessels — "Lady of Mann", "Ben-My-Chree", "Tynwald", "Fenella", "Manxman" and "Viking" — were all engaged in the Dunkirk evacuation. The "Fenella" was lost by enemy action.

Seven naval units likewise perished: the six destroyers H.M.S. "Grafton", "Grenade", "Wakeful", "Basilisk", "Keith", "Havant"; and the Fleet Minesweeper H.M.S. "Skipjack".

The "Brighton Queen", which previously had been engaged minesweeping, arrived off Dunkirk at dawn, sent her boats to fetch soldiers aboard from the beach, then went to the assistance of a motor vessel which had got aground. Having successfully towed her off, this excursion steamer encountered savage attacks from bombers but managed to land her passengers in England.

She then returned to Dunkirk, ran the gauntlet of many more onslaughts, and by her Lewis guns kept the enemy at bay. Having loaded up with more troops — chiefly French and Algerian — she reached the open sea. This time luck was not with her. Again the bombers concentrated a deadly hate, "Brighton Queen" sank to the bottom, though most of her men and all her officers were rescued.

The "Waverley" was a veteran of the last war (having in that period put in four strenuous years of minesweeping). Built so far back as the year 1899, she was reconditioned and returned to service on the Clyde, where many passengers will remember the trips she used to run to Rothesay and elsewhere. Her tragic ending on May 29 came as almost a personal loss to many people who had known "Waverley" all their lives. She died gamely, carrying British soldiers who fired their rifles continuously against the twelve Nazi bombers which flew over and brought the disaster.

The S.S. "St. Seiriol" well exemplifies the grit and pluck which these pleasure craft so nobly possessed. North-country holiday-makers will know that she used to run trips from Llandudno, but they may be interested to learn that to and from Dunkirk she actually made seven trips — one of the best efforts throughout the whole episode. Officers and crew alike were completely played out. Without any sort of rest, subjected also to the immense strain from aerial attack, they finally attained an advanced stage of physical and nervous exhaustion which no layman can describe.

Her Chief Officer, a man of about 60 years and by no means of athletic stature, had spent the whole of one night under circumstances hard enough to fatigue one half his age enjoying full vigour. Three of the ship's boats having been blown away by bombs, he spent the dark hours rescuing survivors from a sunken vessel and actually picked up no fewer than 150 by sheer loyalty to duty. On arrival in port he became partially paralysed below the waist, yet all that he asked was permission to go back and do one more trip.

Mr. R. Thomas, serving as Acting Boatswain in this "St. Seiriol", told me that she had already made three trips to Dunkirk by May 29. She used to send away three boats in charge, respectively, of the Chief Officer, Second Mate, and Boatswain to the dreaded beach, and every time would bring off an average of 47 soldiers in each boat though bombs dropped from the 'planes "as though raining". These troops they transferred to H.M. Destroyers or Drifters lying anchored in the Roads, and then filled up the "St. Seiriol" herself, which averaged about 900 evacuated passengers during all these seven voyages to the Kentish port. Her Master, Captain R. Morris, despite a hot tornado of fire, did not hesitate to take his vessel even within the Dunkirk piers, but discovered that he could much better embark the soldiers whilst anchored a short distance out.

If some ships were unlucky, "St. Seiriol" belonged to the fortunate, though how she survived was a miracle in itself. Often a dozen aircraft flew over simultaneously, circled around to take careful aim with their missiles and raked the decks with machine-gun bullets. As the latter kept bouncing off the hull or tearing up the woodwork, it was a real test for human discipline, especially when this happened thrice in succession; yet although many of the rescued included troops who had just come through hell's yawning mouth, and some sailors hauled out of the sea after losing their vessel, an amazingly cool calm still pervaded. Despite their wounds, these survivors took quite a favourable view of life.

The "St. Seiriol's" seamen vied with firemen and others of the crew in providing their guests with dry clothes, or bedding on which to rest wearied bodies, whilst stewards got busy with supplies of food. Captain Morris informed me that his men exhibited "a remarkable heroism despite the continued and fierce bombing", but forgets that though some were nervously shocked and all came through without a scratch, this was largely by reason of his own fine seamanship.

Now this S.S. "St. Seiriol", owned by the Liverpool and North Wales Steamship Company, which possessed likewise the S.S. "St. Tudno" and the Motorship "St. Silio", became one of the most useful vessels from the first. On Tuesday, May 21, she tried to enter Calais, succeeded in spite of the bombs, getting alongside the quay, and cleared away out of it at 8-30 p.m.

Then on May 27 she went with the Motorship "Queen of the Channel" to Dunkirk and at first was alongside the jetty, but afterwards sent to wait off the beach. She at this date was commanded by Captain R. D. Dobb, with Mr. J. McNamee as Chief Officer. Her boats were invaluable picking up troops from the beach: the first boat in charge of the Second Officer, one A.B. and a fireman; the second boat in charge of an A.B. and a signalman; but the third looked after by the crew of a trawler.

It was a night of very great darkness, though the burning buildings ashore lit up the beach and thereby helped the men ferrying from the beach to the nearest destroyers in the roadstead. The "St. Seiriol", with her lessened crew, was next instructed to reach the jetty, and had to leave her boats still doing their great work. She herself embarked 680 soldiers direct from the land and left about midnight for Dover.

That night "Queen of the Medway" was bombed and sunk.

When "St. Seiriol" on the afternoon of May 29 left Dover for Dunkirk, she at first went alongside the jetty with "Fenella The latter was lying next to the "Crested Eagle", so the Llandudno ship could really make no contact with the shore and came away (as mentioned) believing results more easily obtainable from boats ferrying from the beach.

It was a nocturnal venture when everything that could was exploding in the sky. Mr McNamee said he could only describe it as "a cavalcade of planes" coming over the already damaged harbour and ships being sunk on either side of the jetty. No wonder that "Fenella" was bombed and hit, that the "Crested Eagle", which burned oil-fuel, became by one direct hit a blazing furnace. Deliberately she was run ashore, the "St. Seiriol" lowered the one available boat and under very heavy aerial attack rescued 150 men and gave them First Aid aboard; but many of them were found to be scalded, burned, or half drowned.

The loss of "Crested Eagle" made a deep impression upon the minds of all beholders. As she burst into flames, many men were seen to jump overboard, and as she grounded on the beach it was one white-hot mass that no power could put out. Men from "St. Seiriol" got as close to her as possible, and for about hours were toiling to save men from the horrible holocaust. Some who were picked up without clothing now had to be wrapped in blankets, but all the survivors were kindly looked after by the seamen and given refreshments. Two of the "Crested Eagle's" people eventually died before reaching England.

Meanwhile Mr McNamee had gone to the beach for the B.E.F. wading out towards the boats. He found the discipline wonderful and the leadership by their Army officers perfect. The briefest questions and answers sufficed.

"How many men can you stow in the boat?"

"Ten at a time. Then we come back for some more."

So, with a good push from the lads ashore, the laden boat was sent afloat and the ship could at last weigh anchor for home. But the exceptional courage and endurance of "St. Seiriol" in her trips of May 27 and 29 considerably impressed the naval authorities. Such trips also severely strained and shook this determined crew, so that on arrival at Dover the military doctor decided that both Master and all hands were unfit to carry on in her any longer. They were sent to their homes for a rest and another crew took the ship to continue the brave duty that must ever be associated with this pleasure vessel.

Grievous, and most painful, it was that some of our very best pleasure units had to be sacrificed in this holocaust. Londoners will not easily forgive the Nazis for having destroyed the "Crested Eagle", one of the most beautifully designed hulls that ever used the Thames. Perhaps even in peace time those who used to make excursions with speed to Clacton failed fully to appreciate a product of that Cowes firm famous for the many yachts and destroyers it had launched.

This "Greyhound of the River Thames", as some called her, was a beautiful sight for any genuine shiplover as she sped by driven at full speed by 3500 horse-power; but her sister the "Royal Eagle" was the largest and most luxurious among all the Thames pleasure steamers. Of 1538 tons, she could carry nearly 2000 passengers at 19 knots to Ramsgate, and thus was able to render magnificent service when the B.E.F. had to be fetched off in a hurry. Altogether no fewer than ten ships belonging to the General Steam Navigation Company and its associate organisation the New Medway Steam Packet Company were engaged in the Dunkirk operations; for additional to the "Crested Eagle" and "Royal Eagle" were the "Golden Eagle", "Royal Sovereign", "Royal Daffodil", "Queen of the Channel", "Queen of Thanet", "Medway Queen", "Aboukir", and "Bullfinch".

Further details of their share in these exciting events will be mentioned in due course, but it may be noted in passing that when awards were published they included Commander J. C. K. Dowding, R.D., R.N.R. (commanding officer of "Mona's Isle"), Lieut. A. T. Cook, R.N.R., of "Medway Queen", Mr A. Paterson (Chief Officer of the "Royal Daffodil"), and Captain J. H. Whiteway (Master of the "Tynwald").

War is an ugly business anyway, but it would be impossible to congratulate an enemy for having sunk so beautiful a creature as that twin-screw turbine "Mona's Queen" (2756 tons) in her sixth year of existence.

Pleasure vessels? How ironical the description sounds! What a contrast between purpose and actual fulfilment that whereas these ships in any ordinary June would be affording rest and enjoyment to thousands of happy travellers, they were extricating thousands of harassed anxious warriors whose fate had seemed foredoomed!

As for the officers and crews responsible, many mariners became so utterly fatigued that they could scarcely speak, and some after falling asleep remained unconscious during the next twenty-five hours.

Yet such was the eagerness of one ship's company to go and fetch more men, that she sailed off without waiting for orders.

We mentioned just now the "Queen of the Channel", and the ending to which this motor ship was compelled to go. Let us see how this came about, for "Queen of the Channel" is too well remembered by the public for merely a casual mention. This vessel was requisitioned for Government service as a troop-carrying transport on 8th January, 1940, when lying in the River Fal.

She proceeded to Dover, where she arrived on 15th January and fitted out for the Service. Fitting out was completed on the 20th February, compasses adjusted on the 21st, and the first passage made on the 23rd February to Boulogne with 492 troops returning from leave. Five Lewis guns and also several gunners were attached to the ship for defensive purposes.

The vessel continued in this service fairly regularly during March and April, one voyage being made each day, when she carried on an average about 500 troops per passage, and about 13,000 in all. After leave for troops was stopped, about 1st May, the vessel ran with mails, King's Messenger, and troop details until 18th May. The Irish Guards were carried to Boulogne for final defence of that port, wounded and R.A.M.C. details brought back to Dover on the 22nd May.

On the 19th May a special voyage was commenced to Dunkirk for refugees, but the ship was stopped off Gravelines and eventually returned to Dover without proceeding to Dunkirk.

On 23rd May the vessel proceeded to the Downs anchorage, returning to Dover on the 24th, and anchoring in the outer harbour until the morning of the 27th. The vessel's Lewis guns were in action against enemy aircraft on the nights of the 23rd and 26th.

On the morning of the 27th May at 5 a.m. orders were received to stand by and proceed to Dunkirk. Vessel victualled and watered and she proceeded at 2 p.m. Arrival at Dunkirk was about 8 p.m., making fast to the eastern breakwater. About 50 troops were taken on board, after which the ship was ordered to anchor off the beach and send boats ashore for troops. Four boats were sent away and made several trips bringing off about 200 troops.

Fresh orders were then received to return to the eastern breakwater and complete. Boats were hoisted inboard, except one which could not be traced in the dark. Vessel re-secured to breakwater, the balance of men were taken on board, making a total of about 920, and at 2-55 a.m., on the 28th, proceeded on the return voyage.

During the whole of the time in Dunkirk air raids were in progress, bombs being dropped through thick smoke indiscriminately and several wrecks on the banks being also machine-gunned. Fortunately none fell close to the ship.

After sailing at about 4-15 a.m., half an hour before sunrise, an aeroplane was observed approaching on the starboard bow about 2000 feet up, distinguishing marks not being decipherable. This plane circled and dived when on the port beam. Lewis-gun fire was then opened from the ship, but 3 or 4 bombs had then been released which straddled the ship a little abaft the mainmast. The slight delay action of these bombs caused an upward explosion which broke the vessel's back, the starboard propeller shaft and rudder, the stern dipping into the water. The wireless aerial had also carried away and No. 5 boat was blown across the deck.

Lewis-gun fire was continued as guns were able to bear. The aeroplane again circled and approached the port bow, dropping more bombs which fell about 100 feet away and, after apparently passing through two lines of tracer bullets from the forward two guns, the plane flew away to the eastward.

Meanwhile the aerial had been rehoisted and an S.O.S. sent forth, the four remaining boats swung out, and the troops ordered on the loud speakers to vacate the after end of the ship and walk forward, in order to lighten the after end as much as possible.

A slight electric wire fire was extinguished in the after dining-saloon. Pumps were started on the two after lower saloons. Reports from the carpenter shewed that water was making rapidly in the after four compartments, therefore orders were given to lower away boats and fill them. This work proceeded in good order.

The S.S. "Dorrien Rose", a store ship proceeding to Dunkirk, was standing by and, as the weather was fine, was requested to come alongside forward; the two vessels were secured port bow to starboard bow to prevent troops all going to one side and listing the "Queen of the Channel".

The troops were then ordered over the rail to the other ship, this work proceeded smoothly, the lifeboats meanwhile making an extra passage, having discharged their troops into the "Dorrien Rose".

By 5-20 a.m. all troops had been transferred. A further inspection was made, and water was found to be gaining in the steward's store-room and engine-room, and by this time the bow was out of the water. It was therefore decided to abandon ship. Confidential papers were collected, and final transfer was completed by 5-25.

The "Dorrien Rose" let go and proceeded to Dover, arrival being at 2-30 p.m., and the passage being without further untoward incident, and during part of it one destroyer also acted as escort. The four lifeboats were towed for extra security in case of further attack, but during the passage two broke away and were lost.

It should be added that "Dorrien Rose", a 1350-tons steamer of Cardiff, owned by Messrs Richard Hughes & Co. had made one attempt to approach Dunkirk days previously. On coming from the Downs, she sighted the city in flames, and in passing three outward-bound vessels received from one a signal that it was unsafe to go nearer. Accordingly the "Dorrien Rose" reversed course and came back.

But at 3 a.m., on May 28, towards dawn she again set off and was getting near to the Dunkirk vicinity in daylight when she was off Middlekerke and received onslaught from aircraft, against which she blazed away with her gun. Five o'clock had barely come than she realised that the General Steam Navigation Company's motor ship, "Queen of the Channel", was definitely sinking, so "Dorrien Rose" altered course and went to her assistance.

Even whilst in the act of taking off troops and the stranger's crew, Germans repeatedly sought to renew the attack, but a burst of fire from "Dorrien Rose's" machine-guns prevented this. When all had been safely transferred from "Queen of the Channel" and the "Dorrien Rose" had landed them at Dover, the latter again made for Dunkirk the following night, but at 3 a.m. a new sort of engagement took place. A couple of "E"-boats, better known as motor torpedo craft, circled the ship and sprayed her with machine-guns.

This did not delay "Dorrien Rose" who promptly "gave as good as she received", so that she arrived safely at Dunkirk, landed some valuable stores for the rearguard troops, and came back thence with 590 soldiers for Folkestone.

CHAPTER XI — THE LIFE SAVERS

OF all the contrasted ship types which assisted in the Dunkirk evacuation there was one that had been specially designed and built solely for the purpose of saving lives at sea; yet nobody had ever visualised employment of these special craft collectively and for the same purpose.

It was not till the afternoon of Thursday, May 30, that a telephone message from the Ministry of Shipping to the Royal National Lifeboat Institution made a request for as many lifeboats as possible to be sent immediately for service under the Admiral commanding at Dover.

A pretty big demand, when you consider that "immediately" would include that district so far north as Norfolk and so far west as Dorset. The modern introduction of motors has, of course, given the lifeboat an independent mobility and range of action that would have been beyond all possibility in the days of oars and sails; yet it meant no small evidence of good organisation that, although most of this Thursday was finished, there were collected in Dover Harbour that day or on Friday no fewer than seventeen.

Another remarkable fleet!

These came from the following stations: Great Yarmouth, Gorleston, Lowestoft, Aldeburgh (2 boats), Walton and Frinton, Clacton, Southend-on-Sea, Walmer, Hythe, Dungeness, Hastings, Eastbourne, Newhaven, Shoreham, Poole. This made sixteen, but it so happened that a motor life-boat having been just completed for Cadgwith, she was despatched direct to Dover from the builders' yard at Rowhedge.

On arrival at the assembly port, the R.N.L.I. crews were replaced by naval ratings, except that both Ramsgate and Margate boats (working under the direct orders of naval officers in command at these two places) were manned by their own crews and went straight to Dunkirk. The Dover life-boat was not sent to France, because the Admiralty already had ear-marked her for their own use for the many duties at this port.

It is regrettable that no records exist of the fine work which these craft performed, but activities were more essential than reports at that time. From conversations with officers who commanded life-boats I derived the impression that the most outstanding recollections were of the heavy pall of smoke enveloping Dunkirk, the chaotic medley of craft within its harbour moving about in the darkness and each trying desperately hard to avoid collision; the tragic spectacle of ships ashore, the bedlam of bangs from overhead, the wonderful discipline of embarking soldiers.

If Dunkirk was the prerogative of no particular age, with the most heterogeneous assortment of men and vessels, it showed a combination thoroughly international. If there were Dutch *schuyts*, which only a few weeks previously carried out their daily avocation under Netherlandish colours but now were in charge of young British naval officers and flew the White Ensign as H.M. Skoots, there likewise assisted Belgian trawlers which had rushed across from Ostend to England, French fishing smacks, British oyster dredgers from Essex.

But the familiar blue-hulled life-boats somehow looked the strangest visitors in foreign waters. Aboard the Ramsgate and Margate two boats were crews whose ages aggregated 600, yet you may judge from the following whether these men of 'riper years' contributed their full share in the great undertaking.

It was at 2-20 p.m. of May 30 that the Ramsgate boat left England towing eight wherries, which on arrival off the French beach landed tins of drinking water and began fetching off troops. The latter were transferred to the life-boat, and then carried to a motor ship waiting in the Roads. Altogether 800 soldiers were thus rescued that night. The motor ship, however, was having some trouble with her engine, so two of the Ramsgate men went aboard and helped bring her home to our southeast coast, whilst the reduced life-boat crew remained off Dunkirk and continued embarking soldiers throughout the day and night of Friday the 31st until the last of the wherries had been destroyed.

The boat then made for her own port, having been working under heavy fire all the while. You may call it luck, or good seamanship — or both; but the remarkable fact emerges that not one of this Ramsgate crew became a casualty, and their life-boat though somewhat scarred was really very little damaged. Altogether she had been able to evacuate 2800 men. Barely was she back on her station after a 'wash and brush up' than at daybreak of June 5 two small craft were reported showing blankets on their spars, so out went the Ramsgate life-saver again. She found a small motor craft towing a ship's oared boat barely able to stem the strong tide.

Sixty-eight French *poilus*, who had escaped from Dunkirk at 6 o'clock on the morning of June 4 — all of them without food or water, and none of them possessing the slightest seafaring knowledge — were not far from fatigue after fighting Nazis to the last hour and suffering the uncertainties of their voyaging. Fortunately, someone among these evacuees managed to get the motor running, but any Kentish mariner could have told them that by all the rules of chance the two boats should have been wrecked on the Goodwins.

The Margate life-boat, which likewise left for Dunkirk on that Thursday afternoon, May 30, was towed thither. Between shore and waiting destroyers she made six or seven exciting trips, carrying off nearly 600 soldiers, but by 7-15 next morning the wind had piped up and sent such a vicious swell on to the beach that it was impossible to carry on, so she laid a course for Margate, and this permitted her to achieve another valuable bit of work. For, on the way, she came across an open boat containing seventeen officers and men who might have perished among the waves; but now the blue benefactor was able to snatch them from an awkward predicament.

In those days the lookouts from southeastern England might expect any sort of craft at any hour of the day or night. For among those hundreds of thousands who had marched towards Dunkirk must be some stragglers who, having missed their transport, would scrounge around till they found some stray boat without a hole in her. The Dover life-boat twice made herself useful and fulfilled her original purpose. The first time was during the night of June 2 when she went out to bring in a disabled motor-boat drifting towards the Goodwins helplessly. Fifteen exhausted British soldiers thus had reason to express their gratitude.

Three days afterwards, in the early morning, she fetched into harbour fifteen more warriors who had been rowing all the way from Dunkirk since the previous day and could not have held out much longer. Two were Belgian, thirteen were French, and never did 'perfidious Albion's' white cliffs seem so beautiful with return of daylight.

On such an occasion as this Dunkirk operation, when the British Army's very existence depended on a miracle, no one could reckon up the cost in sterling. Human lives, prestige, national security, cannot be considered by any monetary standards. The actual cost of this huge assemblage of vessels amounted to an incredible sum, even omitting the expense of purely naval units or the losses of valuable hulls. The figures representing cost of fuel, food, equipment, and incidentals, would alone appal any accountant.

As a slight indication of this colossal enterprise it may be mentioned that the expense to the R.N.L.I. amounted to £8000, which included loss of their Hythe life-boat, replacement of equipment and stores, repairs, and so on. Of course the Institution refused to let the nation pay one penny and resolved themselves to bear all charges. The Eastbourne life-boat was damaged severely so that she had to be abandoned, yet later came back and was taken in hand by the shipwrights. Practically all the others suffered injuries of some degree.

But how small a price to pay in the long fight for Europe's freedom! How little it will mean some day when we have won a righteous victory!

Had not the enterprise been so terribly serious one might have likened these thousands of Channel crossings to one tremendous regatta, in which the Navy, Mercantile Marine, fishermen and yachtsmen were all racing against each other to make the greatest number of trips and rescue the largest crowd.

Certainly a healthy rivalry — on the pride-of-ship principle — did nothing but good. One destroyer made five consecutive journeys through a hail of shells and bombs, till on the sixth trip the damage inside her engine-room reduced her speed to half. Despite this she then made a seventh, and this time survived three dive-bomb assaults by a hundred warplanes.

In contrast to her an old man of 70 years with a boy went ambling along in his slow motorboat. A naval pensioner, accustomed to hard knocks, he could not bear to think any of our soldiers might be left behind, so backwards and forwards during three days and nights he went to Dunkirk's shell-pitted beach. Then on the seventh occasion, just as his open boat was between two breakwaters and the wash from other ships' propellers lashed the water into pyramids, one wave leapt aboard, filled her, and down she sank. This entrance, one experienced officer told me, was a veritable nightmare in the dark, comparable only to crossing a railway when express trains are rushing in each direction.

As we reconstruct in our minds those prolonged hours, our wonder becomes greater that anything human survived. Rescuing vessels seemed hedged about with danger all the while. If they skirted the minefields, they came under attack from shore guns: if by a bit of luck, or cleverness, these were dodged, then the dive-bombers had to be reckoned with. Little wonder that even small targets were sunk, and many more damaged. Very few of the larger craft escaped harm from the air, and none got through their duties without most terrifying danger.

As at the Battle of Jutland, there was a 'windy corner', so throughout these ten days ships dreaded a certain spot where course had to be altered and in so doing they must feel the concentrated strength of the enemy's guns. With steady, rhythmic firing the Germans registered exactly on the target. So many seconds ... then bang ... so many seconds, and another shell. In course of time the more observant commanding officers eased engines before reaching this pivot and counted the number of seconds till the flash came; then, by suddenly accelerating speed, ships might just pass round the corner between the falling of one shot and the next.

During the last war a number of steam yachts belonging to wealthy owners were taken up by the Admiralty and performed service in different parts of Europe, especially against submarines. One such was H.M. Yacht "Narcissus" (commanded by a retired British admiral), whose guns so damaged UB-49 one autumn day that the German had to make for Cadiz. When in 1939 this Second European War started, steam yachts had become comparatively few: some had been sold abroad, others broken up, but the old "Narcissus" was still afloat. Furthermore she returned to fly the White Ensign, and though she became known as H.M.S. "Grive" (a Fleet Air Arm tender) there could be no mistaking her personality.

The admiral had long since passed away, but another not less gallant officer emerged from retirement and took over. This was Lord Cavan's brother, Captain the Hon. Lionel Lambart, D.S.O., R.N., and you can understand a man by his recreations no less than by his physical trials. As a Sub-Lieutenant he had all his toes crushed in a gunnery accident and completely severed from one foot, yet despite excruciating pain that youngster bore it without a murmur, grew up, continued his naval career.

When the time came to retire, he was still a famous polo-player and a hard rider to hounds, who knew neither fear nor the limit of endurance. Then he took up flying, and at the age of 60, when most men select a quieter life, qualified as an air pilot. Courteous, gentle, musical, loathing any sort of self-advertisement, he came back to his old service at 67 and was given command of H.M.S. "Grive". In this 816 tons yacht he performed magnificent work. Although such a vessel was neither young nor spacious, he enabled her during three hectic days and nights to rescue no less than 2000 of the B.E.F. Then at last on her fourth trip to Dunkirk the enemy sank her, himself, and most of her crew of forty-three, though Sub-Lieut. J. K. B. Miles, R.N.V.R., survived and received the D.S.C.

We mentioned just now the fact of Dutch vessels taking part, and it is sufficient commentary of their usefulness that British naval officers serving in H.M. Skoots "Doggers-bank", "Hondsrug", "Twente" and "Hilda" were among those who afterwards earned decorations. The Dutch Navy also was represented in this withdrawal and lost one of its ships, though that by no means represented the full gallant effort on the part of that Service.[3]

There is an old saying that 'sailors look after each other' regardless of nationality, and this statement would not wholly exclude some of the North German types if only their political leaders could be dismissed. For, barely a year prior to this second war, I remember in foreign waters being paid a courtesy from such a one that was as spontaneous as welcome, though most of us would need considerable proof before agreeing that any Nazi airman or soldier would be so humanly minded.

But what could be more self-sacrificing than the behaviour of those three Fleetwood fishermen, whose gallantry won them each a medal of the O.B.E.? Immediately after their trawler "Gava" arrived in Fleetwood after a fishing trip, the entire crew volunteered to go on for Dunkirk. Not one of them had previously been under fire, but that did not worry them. The "Gava" carried one 12-pdr. and a Bren gun.

If you've been shipmates with fishermen, you will know that even a 3-pdr. makes them superlatively happy and confident because they can show their pluck by hitting hard at the enemy. Now, whilst off the French coast, the "Gava" proved that Nazi aviators were not such clever rulers of the sky as some pretended. The trawlermen blazed away and, with that accuracy of aim for which they were noted in the last war, brought down three German 'planes, and possibly a fourth.

Many a regular man-of-war would have been proud of such gunnery: but the "Gava" had not finished.

She steamed alongside Dunkirk jetty, received 376 French soldiers, went just outside and in the roadstead hove-to for the purpose of rescuing survivors from a French destroyer that had been sunk. Three sailors were sighted in the sea almost at the end of their struggle for life. Instantly three of "Gava's" people, without shedding a garment, dived overboard. They were young fellows — John Jones, a 23-year old deckhand; Harry Gawne, 27, another deckhand; and Arthur Dunne, of the same age, wireless operator. To their brave efforts, in spite of the sluicing tideway, the Frenchmen owe gratitude for being hoisted from death.

Skipper Fred Day then noticed that another armed trawler, having broken down, with 123 survivors on board from the destroyer, was in real danger. "Gava" therefore went alongside her, added the 123 to the 3 others which made 126 plus 376 or a total of 499, which must be a record for any ship of her size.

It is strange how often that, despite human anxiety, things have a way of regulating themselves far better than we could contrive.

When the decision had to be made for utilising Dunkirk, with its narrow entrance, comparatively shallow and restricted approach, many of us felt uneasy knowing that any evacuation would be a long and slow business because there could be no opportunity for any big transport capable of carrying say 5000 at a time. But, looking back, we can rejoice exceedingly that our troops were spread over many and small vessels rather than bunched together in a few of considerable tonnage.

Far preferable, indeed, that there should be a vast array of little ships instead of a few immense targets which no enemy airman could fail to hit. And one officer told me that as he entered Dunkirk harbour on the night of May 31 he found the acrid smoke not a hindrance but a protective screen, because the wind's direction blew along this curtain till it hung parallel with the shore.

But consider the report made by Captain H. Buxton of the 433 tons motorship "Bullfinch", owned by the General Steam Navigation Company. She had, previous to hostilities, been normally engaged trading with Northern France.

"At 10.20 p.m. on 28th May 1940, whilst at anchor in Small Downs, the m.v. 'Bullfinch' received orders to sail at once for La Panne beaches. The ship arrived off the beaches about 4.50 a.m. on May 29th. The beach was crowded with troops, but there were only a few boats bringing off small numbers. The Master received orders to beach the 'Bullfinch' and accordingly he let go the Kedge anchor and headed slow for the beach.

The vessel grounded about 5.43 a.m., but owing to the Kedge anchor not holding, her stern swung to the eastward and the ship was aground fore and aft with the beach.

"After the first boatload came aboard one of the troops swam ashore with a line. Two 5-inch ropes were run ashore and hauled boats off and back to the beach. When the tide receded the troops waded off and embarked up the ship's ladders. Embarkation proceeded until the ship had about 1300 on board, during which time the ballast tanks were pumped out. The ladders were then pulled up, as the ship could take no more.

"The troops had two Bren guns with them which were mounted one each side of the boat deck. The troops also manned the ship's Lewis gun. Bomb attacks were taking place all day and, after a very anxious time from 5.30 p.m. until 6.15 p.m., the vessel floated and proceeded.

"German aircraft attacked the ship repeatedly. When passing Dunkirk several bombs dropped close to the vessel's stern, the concussion from which caused the circuit breaker to come out and put the steering gear out of action. The engines were stopped whilst the Engineers effected repairs and the ship then proceeded.

"Three dive bombers then attacked the 'Bullfinch' from aft. One of the Bren gunners, Sergeant Cook, shot one down into the sea. Shortly afterwards three others attacked from forward and the Sergeant again shot one down. Further attacks were made at frequent intervals until a formation of Spitfires drove the enemy off.

"On arrival in the Small Downs the 'Bullfinch' received orders to proceed to Ramsgate Harbour, where the troops were promptly disembarked.

"It was afterwards discovered that the concussion from the exploding bombs had put both compasses out. The ship was on one occasion attacked by machine-gun fire but only one soldier was wounded. The Master of the 'Bullfinch' stated that he could not speak too highly of the Bren Gunner, who held his fire until the 'planes were close to the vessel and undoubtedly saved the ship."

The "Golden Eagle", as we know, was originally a passenger ship and for that reason became exactly suited for transferring troops from France to England. In years to come, when most of us are dead and ships which made themselves famous are long since broken up, people will still wish to read authentic accounts of the officers responsible for driving these vessels in and out of that terrible tornado of death. It is therefore well that we should present the account of Mr. F. Barnes, Chief Engineer of the "Golden Eagle". He says:

"We carried about 2000 troops over from Dunkirk.

"On our first trip we came up to the survivors of the 'Waverley', which had just been bombed and sunk. They were in the water and had been machine gunned after the ship had sunk. With so many of the men wounded and exhausted, we returned to Margate to land them.

"The next time we arrived off the beach east of Dunkirk at 8 a.m. and left at 9 p.m. It was a slow job getting men off the beach, with only the two boats belonging to the ship. We were attacked on and off all the time by bombers, but our pom-poms appeared to hold them off each time until fighters arrived. We eventually had to leave our position off the beach, owing to heavy artillery fire. An aeroplane was overhead spotting for the guns. Finally we went inside the harbour and filled up with troops. There were about 1500 on board. While inside the harbour an attack was made with about 50 'planes. Although a number of ships were alongside the pier none were hit, but bombs fell uncomfortably close.

"The last time we went was at night. We were ordered to be alongside the east pier at 1 a.m. The ship arrived off Dunkirk at that time, and we did not go in until 3 a.m. The order had been given to retire when we were told to go in and get what we could, but be out again by 2.50 a.m. We got inside and alongside the pier, but got nobody. The block ships then came in and told us to get out. The shelling was very heavy and I think we were very fortunate not to be hit. In getting away one of the sponson springs was caught in the port wheel.

"We stopped outside to clear it. The loose was got out but it was tightly bound around the banjo with so many turns that it would have taken a long time to cut away. We were the only ship in the roads except a destroyer, all others having gone. With daylight breaking and shells getting close the only thing to do was to chance it. The wheel made a lot of noise, the grease pipe carried away and the banjo was rather warm when we got back, but it did get us back."

CHAPTER XII — THE RAILWAY STEAMERS

SINCE the distance between Dunkirk and Dover is so short that in peace time the ferry service traversed it in only four hours, we can quite understand that such vessels as railway steamers accustomed to make quick crossings from Dover to Calais, Newhaven to Dieppe, Folkestone to Boulogne, or Holyhead to Ireland, were exceptionally suited for the withdrawal of the B.E.F.

Space, speed, moderate draught were the most desirable essentials, so that a 21-knots Dover-Calais packet by fulfilling these conditions exactly should be found fairly ideal for such naval undertaking. This was proved in actual experience for, whereas soldiers aboard a destroyer were packed so tightly that they slept whilst standing up, not more than 1200 could be usually carried at a time; the Dover-Calais railway steamers every trip were able to bring 2000 troops, land them quickly, and then go back for more.

The resourcefulness and endurance of these master mariners was beyond all praise, even when suddenly called from their normal routes to navigate unfamiliar and decidedly tricky waters. It will best illustrate alike their skill and difficulties if we select one of these typical voyages made during the very height of the withdrawal.

The L.M. & Scottish Railway Company's S.S. "Scotia" was lying off Southampton at two hours' notice on May 27 when at 7-30 p.m. she received orders to make for Dover "with all possible speed". By 9-30 p.m. she started, arrived off Dover at 7 a.m. May 28, and that evening at 5 o'clock left the Downs for Dunkirk, the weather being calm and hazy.

In the approaches to the latter she found a number of our destroyers anchored, and busily shelling the enemy's positions. It was an impressive experience for the most travelled seafarers — night settling down, Dunkirk's city all ablaze, dense smoke obscuring the port, violent explosions inside, heavy guns booming from the shore.

Midnight passed, but five minutes before one o'clock "Scotia" felt a thud. Something struck her abaft the engine-room, port side. Something heavy.

They sounded, but soon reassured themselves she was making no water. A marvellous escape! She had been hit by a torpedo against the bilge keel, and the missile had failed to explode.

"Is Dunkirk clear?" Captain W. H. Hughes hailed a small sloop.

And about 1-30 a.m. reassured, "Scotia" berthed close to the lighthouse on the East Pier. Along marched 3000 Britons in khaki, thoroughly exhausted, and many of them so weary that they could hardly drag their legs. But the Embarkation Officers who had been on duty thirty-six hours without a break rivalled them for fatigue.

A new day was just dawning as "Scotia" came out again to sea, with saddening sights revealing themselves in the pale gleam: a destroyer lying wrecked, a troopship of the tramp class badly ashore and now disembarking her passengers into several small craft.

Yes: the "Scotia" was carrying the full limit and even more, so that when after six hours she tried coming alongside Dover's landing quay it was most difficult, owing to the heavy list shoreward by the soldier crowds eager to land.

After steaming next to coal at Sheerness, she was off again for more thrills. They were waiting around Dunkirk. "Windy off number so-and-so buoy", a passing destroyer signalled as warning, but a sloop in tow with smoke issuing fore and aft emphasised this liveliness. Presently the sloop had to be abandoned.

And now ten German bombers were seen making directly towards "Scotia", but the latter from Bren gun on poop deck and Lewis gun by the navigating bridge opened fire. What with that, engines going full speed, and Captain Hughes' clever use of the helm, not one of the bombs hit. Very characteristic of the way in which the Nazi 'planes sought to avoid combat was the fact that when presently several British aircraft were seen approaching from the northeast, the enemy promptly disappeared only to return when ours had passed over. "We were now approaching Dunkirk", relates Captain Hughes, "steering inside the channel buoys so as to avoid wrecks, fully occupied trying to avoid these and the buoys. I had reduced speed approaching the entrance, when the Germans again dropped two bombs, one about 100 feet from the port quarter, the other about 50 feet ahead of us."

Arriving at the West Mole by n a.m., the "Scotia" discovered the place quiet except for a few rounds from the Nazi shore batteries, yet no time was unnecessarily wasted. In less than half an hour 2000 French troops had been embarked and the ship started back.

Good going? Yes: but the enemy thought this to be his big chance.

Rushing up from astern, twelve aeroplanes in fours swooped low, the two outside ones spluttering bullets and the two inner ones each dropping four bombs, but again they failed to find a target. The second formation of four sent their bullets all round the bridge, the funnels, and in the water ahead; one bomb falling on the ship abaft her engine-room on the starboard side, another striking the poop deck. When the third four came low, one bomb — incredible though it may sound — fell down the after funnel, and a second hit the stern.

That was a most serious matter.

The Captain sent out one 'S.O.S.', ordered another to be despatched, but learned that the wireless cabin had been shattered and the operator blown out though escaping any hurt. Alas! "Scotia" was damaged badly, sinking by the stern, heeling over to starboard, doomed, and her engines put out of action.

"Abandon ship!"

Of the ten life-boats usually carried, three had been smashed by the enemy; moreover, the excitable French could not understand the orders given in English, but started to rush the boats. This made it very difficult for the British sailors to man the falls, especially those on the port side since "Scotia" was heeling to starboard. The vessel's chief officer was doing his best to restore order when a French Army officer thrust a revolver into his hands.

That language the *poilus* understood more easily, then Captain Hughes' mouth whistle and hand-signs calmed them till they stood aside and permitted the boats to be lowered.

Now Lieut.-Commander R. J. H. Couch, R.N., of H.M.S. "Esk", whilst lying in Dunkirk had picked up that 'S.O.S.', and hurried his destroyer to sea at full speed. He found the "Scotia" so far turned over that her boat deck was in the water and the capsize getting worse. With no little skill he pressed the destroyer's bow close to the transport's fo'c'sle head, took off many troops, rescued hundreds from the sea, then cleverly backed out till "Esk" came amidships on the starboard side, his stem being now against the other's boat-deck whilst he continued rescuing more survivors.

The former railway steamer now presented a terrible picture. She had lurched right over until forward funnel and mast were touching the sea, when two other aeroplanes thought it a fine sport to drop four more bombs on a sinking ship, and machine-gun those swimming precariously or clinging desperately to wreckage. The "Esk" was busy enough, but she drove away the Nazis by gunfire. Commander Couch again brilliantly handled his ship, despite the fact that the "Scotia" was so far over that her bilge keel showed up at the port side, on which hundreds of French soldiers were huddled in terror. Some the destroyer hauled aboard by ropes, others dived and swam to her.

Again the bombers returned to continue their dastardly work, and again the "Esk" barked at them and brought one fluttering down. By this time, thanks to the timely naval help, all left the wreck except the "Scotia's" steward, two French soldiers — the three being badly wounded — and Captain Hughes himself.

Then, to the last, it was British seamanship once more upholding its glorious traditions when everything was so disheartening. A rope having been thrown from the destroyer, Captain Hughes secured it round the suffering steward, and by means of a boat fall he was able to lower the steward, easing the jerk into the water and against the warship's side. So at least one of the damaged three managed to be transferred.

"Very badly injured, he was most patient and never grumbled," said this faithful Master of his men; though the poor fellow later had to have his leg amputated.

The two French soldiers were rescued in a similar way. Then, convinced that no other living people remained on what once was "Scotia", Captain Hughes seized hold of a boat-spar swung across from "Esk" and so climbed aboard. Other destroyers came along and boats from another transport likewise assisted, so the net result was that after they had been hurried across to England there were 28 of "Scotia's" crew missing, two others subsequently died in hospital, but 300 troops perished.

At a later date Lieut.-Commander Couch received the D.S.C.; the "Scotia's" Chief Officer, Mr. E. R. Pritchard, who had handled the troops with tact and calmed down their panic did splendidly; though the Chief Engineer lost his life in devotion to duty when "Scotia" went down.

"My crew," said Captain Hughes in admiration, "excelled themselves."

And of their own Master Mariner the crew spoke not less enthusiastically. Of such is the British Merchant Navy composed.

The First War with Germany in 1914-1918 drew the Merchant Navy and Royal Navy together by cords of mutual sympathy, creating a respect for each other's qualities: ever since those years the two branches of seafarers have learnt to understand and regard themselves as brothers. But this Second War has done more than that, and knit them tightly to one indissoluble unity which transcends mere brotherhood. Never have these two services co-operated more closely to the national good, never have they assisted each other to such high purpose.

We are not ungrateful that the Germans, as a common foe, have helped thus much.

But let us look at another of these 'safety-first' railway steamers entering the most dangerous duties with which circumstance has ever threatened Captains who pride themselves on their fine records.

It was on May 28, at 6-30 p.m., that the London & North Eastern Ry. Co.'s "Prague" set out from the Downs in company with the Isle of Man S.S. "Manxman" and the Southern Railway Co.'s "Paris". The latter is so familiar to cross-Channel tourists as to require little enough description, though in this Second War she was serving as a hospital ship and bore the customary markings of such. This fact is stressed because, flouting all international rules, the Nazis exercised no respect for the Geneva Cross.

That night was one of those drizzly, misty, occasions, and it was decided that their course for Dunkirk should be via the Zuydcoote Pass. Those of us who have navigated this channel know that it is narrow, somewhat shallow, and that the tide sets not up and down but athwart it. In clear weather and peace time it is moderately well marked, but not much of a place at night time and with a war on, though its southwestern end is quite near to Dunkirk entrance.

Captain Baxter of "Prague", knowing that his vessel was drawing over 16 feet, and the other two ships much less, wisely resolved that these should take precedence, and so the trio steamed roughly in single-line-ahead.

The night's conditions were certainly not favourable for such craft using such a Pass. But orders are orders. Visibility was distinctly poor, and when near the Zuydcoote it was noticed that most of the buoys were unlit. This might have mattered little had it been broad daylight, for at the southern end I have always found a long conspicuous building on the shore an excellent landmark.

In the darkness, however, both the "Manxman" and "Paris" ran aground, and the "Prague" just touched. You can imagine the annoyance and anxiety of mariners, with a clean record and familiar with their own particular 'run', compelled to risk their ships in this fashion. However, "Paris" soon came off, "Manxman" stuck hard and fast for some hours, but Captain Baxter, believing that his steamer drew too much water, retired in the direction of Nieuport and let go anchor to let the tide rise a few feet. He was not alone in this precaution, being later joined by "Manxman".

At 3-55 a.m., one hour before sunrise, they got under way again, had no difficulty in seeing their course through the Pass, and reached Dunkirk, High Water at the latter port being about 5-16 a.m. It was obviously essential that if they were to come back the same way, "Prague" must lose no time. So, having secured to the end of the east jetty, she at once commenced embarking troops. By the time this job was completed, "Prague" drew about 17 ft. 6 in., and at 7-35 a.m. sailed before the tide should drop too much.

Luckily the Pass was negotiated satisfactorily, and after 5½ hours' trip she landed her valuable cargo at Folkestone safely. Next day she spent coaling and watering, and in the evening made a fast trip to Dunkirk. Starting off in a dense fog, she found the weather off the French coast fine and clearer, but alongside the eastern jetty she knew that only 10 ft. of water would be possible at low tide. Again she hurried the embarkation, but when fully loaded and ready to sail on May 30, the tide had fallen so much she would not budge. Finally, only after using both engines at full power, requisitioning also a couple of tugs, enduring considerable shell-fire all round her, the "Prague" got under way and did one more safe trip to Folkestone.

Then her good fortune changed utterly.

Making one more trip to Dunkirk on the first of June, she reached there soon after seven o'clock in the morning. A tall ship like that towered high above the congested harbour, which was badly crowded with smaller wrecks and all sorts of small craft. It was getting near high tide as her hull rose beyond the land and it were useless for the passengers to attempt the usual gangways, so they managed to clamber aboard by planks and the ordinary wooden-runged ladders.

Of course the aeroplanes annoyed her, especially when engaged in the difficult art of berthing such a tall vessel along the western side of the Outer Harbour close by the locks; yet despite this annoyance she kept up a fire from Lewis and Bren guns and succeeded in loading 3000 French troops in about two hours, then left for England. Not always, but generally, it was the French who came aboard from the west side and the English from the other, but it was no mean achievement thus to have accomplished in that time.

On the way back the Gravelines batteries opened up a well directed shell-fire, to make matters more difficult. In such a narrow channel it was impossible for the "Prague" to keep zigzagging, but she went at it full speed, although the shells fell dangerously near.

Then, a little later, when near the Ruytingen the bombers resolved not to let so fine a ship escape, and delivered an intense attack. Six of them dived down from the sky, and even now the other eluding vessels in the neighbourhood returned a brisk answer. But suddenly a lonely aircraft appeared out of the clouds directly overhead, swung round and made directly for the "Prague". The time, 10-25 a.m.

Captain Baxter accordingly starboarded his helm hard as the aircraft released three bombs all together, but from a considerable height. They fell close to the ship's stern just as she was swinging to port, and the explosion was something terrific, the ship being lifted almost out of the water.

An examination proved that the "Prague" had not been hit, though it was quite clear that she had sustained very bad injuries aft. Her stern began to settle down, her starboard shaft was bumping so badly that the engine this side had to be stopped, and although the watertight doors (in accord with war-time practice) had been previously closed, they had been much distorted through the explosion. In effect, the sea filled up to the after engine bulkhead, and water rose to the level of the main deck; one fireman was missing: presumably he had been blown right overboard.

Even now the "Prague" did not give up the encounter. She kept going ahead on her port engine only, and still the water gained. Once more she was able to call up help, and once more it was a destroyer which came to the merchantman's aid; for H.M.S. "Shikari" (a destroyer), together with a sloop and a paddle steamer, in turn came alongside her, which took some doing, as the "Prague" was yet under way nor deemed it advisable to stop. Indeed, the stricken vessel was heading at her very best pace towards the Downs.

Gradually all these 3000 Frenchmen, except a handful, were transferred to the three assisting ships; by 1-30 p.m. the "Prague" had got within the Downs and had called up the well-known tug "Lady Brassey", which made fast a rope. Very gently they beached the "Prague" that afternoon north of Deal, laid a kedge anchor astern, and, after pumping operations and temporary repairs had occupied most of a week, she was towed again by "Lady Brassey" six days later and brought for a complete overhaul into the West India Dock.

The enemy had been robbed of his prey after all.

It is quite natural that apart from the magnificent achievements of our Armed Forces in this Dunkirk Evacuation, the public has been especially thrilled by the adaptability of the pleasure craft and the multiplicity of small yachts and boats.

We shall be, however, historically incorrect not to emphasise the transportation from jetties and beaches by these vessels of the cross-Channel type. So to say, they were of considerable size, though of moderate draught and extremely handy. This was because they had been designed and built for wasting no time in berthing, or departing from more or less shallow harbours.

But the personal element demanded particular attention because the Dunkirk "show" was to last several days, rather than a few hours. Powerful turbines or Diesel engines cannot be entrusted except to the well tried, and the regular engine-room crews must eventually be given some respite. It was there that the various marine societies collaborated for the one big aim. There was, for instance, the Shipping Federation, which represented the shipping owners, being responsible for the supply of crews; and in this it works with the National Union of Seamen. There were likewise the Navigating and Engineer Officers usually engaged by the shipowner direct, but the Shipping Federation in this as on other occasions was called upon to assist with the engagement of officers.

Thus all were able to lend their organisations wholeheartedly — whether of the Owners, the Officers, or the Men — for this unique occasion.

But the cross-Channel packets were in a class by themselves. Ordinarily in peace time their personnel were doing regular trips between termini, and they had been taken over with the ships early in hostilities for the generally frequent transportation of troops across to France. Soon after the special Dunkirk development it was quite obvious that almost indescribable physical and mental strain was being demanded, and that casualties could not be avoided. Relief crews must be supplied extensively, and it was here that the Shipping Federation was able to answer at once the Ministry of Shipping's call.

Dover being in normal times entirely given to cross-Channel work, with regular crews serving in the same ships, it was necessary to send down a staff thither under Captain N. A. Moore, who co-operated with the naval authorities so that from London or other centres relief crews should arrive suitable for each packet. If the men could not instantly be given jobs aboard, they were temporarily billeted. But the great thing was to be ready for taking the place of their opposite numbers who, from exhaustion or injury, could no longer carry on.

It was an excellent idea, one that showed splendid imagination, but there were immense difficulties in the execution. As the reader so well understands from these chapters, the transport from Dunkirk was given barely time to turn round than away she sped to fetch another few hundred troops. Masters, Officers, and Men were so worn out they had to be led ashore, and a Federation official made a rapid survey of the minimum numbers requisite for sending the vessel to sea again.

Men were recruited usually in London, and sent down to Dover by the quickest available method. At such a time the ordinary train service was being worked to the full, so at short notice motor coaches and private cars had to be requisitioned, and billeting in Dover became a serious problem.

How could highly technical engineers be found, suitable for running turbine machinery? And how could these reliefs be discovered at short notice?

Well, it is a tribute to our national organisations that the right men were forthcoming immediately. An appeal for volunteers made in a number of engineering shops met with an overwhelming response. Backed by the complete enthusiasm of their employers, engineers with sea experience left their jobs without even going home. They put on their hats and stepped into the coach.

That which is still more wonderful waits to be mentioned. These men direct from shops and yards walked straight aboard ships, dived below, and took immediate control so that the machinery was soon humming bound for Dunkirk where the soldiers waited. Let me give one instance.

On June 2, just before the culmination of affairs, crews were breaking down right and left: an urgent call was made to send relief officers and men to Dover. Being a Sunday afternoon, the London dock areas had to be scoured, taxis sent to the different works, and from one firm alone there had been collected by 7-30 p.m. 11 officers and 76 men who all had to reach Dover by special coaches. That they were all volunteering for a particularly dangerous adventure they understood. The nation should be ever grateful, the Army cannot but feel thankful, that there were such men ready to 'down tools' and come over to help. The nett result was that no ship of the Merchant Navy was delayed by any shortage of crew, though that is not to say all who needed a rest were given such. One can only marvel that officers and men aboard these ships by an indomitable spirit refused to give in, though nature clearly hinted collapse to be imminent.

We must, then, not forget the auxiliary aid of these self-effacing volunteers who so largely contributed to the ultimate success.

CHAPTER XIII — THE SHIPS CARRY ON

IT is true that the Dunkirk evacuation, which on paper had seemed a wholly impracticable proposition as a large-scale operation, came as a direct answer to national prayer. There can be no question of its being a miraculous intervention.

But we have not yet had time to appreciate alike the Navy's wonderful work nor the equally silent share of the Mercantile Marine's duty in this stupendous undertaking. In particular we are addressing ourselves to the latter before recollection perishes and as a slight memorial to men who toiled till their ships were gone, and their crews were either blown to atoms or human nerves could sustain no longer.

The marvellous feature is that untrained personnel should so readily, and so completely, have accustomed themselves to perform that which was not their original task. By avocation and years of experience they were to attain something quite unordinary, something totally different, and in waters that were unfamiliar.

How can we explain this consummate success other than by the frank admission that throughout the years of steaming they had always been ready for the greatest of all encounters? That fog and storm, navigational difficulties, had bred in these men the very qualities which were demanded off Dunkirk? Captains pitifully but courageously saw their beloved ships sunk despite their best efforts, tricky routes were encumbered with every sort of obstacle, yet still backwards and forwards they carried on making one trip after another.

Look at it in another way. Supposing these ships and men had not been available, supposing there had not been a regular series of cross-Channel packets in existence, how would this have been possible? How, if there had been neither coasters nor paddlers, would it have been within the sphere of anybody to create a service to help remove those thousands of soldiers from the tightest comer in Europe?

We must never thereafter consider the simplest mercantile effort, the lowliest sort of tramp transport, or even the essentially pleasure steamer, except as a cause for deepest admiration and encouragement. We have relied upon them in the past, we look to all these men and their vessels in the future for playing the national duty of seafaring, no matter what their special attributes may be. Too light-heartedly we have accepted in peace time what they have done for us, too easily we have gone aboard night steamers and thought nothing of the skill which by morning has brought us to our destination.

When, for instance, on May 30, in the very height of that Evacuation Week, the London, Midland & Scottish Co.'s S.S. "Princess Maud" left Dover with all speed by the shortest route, she possessed the barest uncertainties of what might befall her ere completing the voyage.

It was hazy weather, visibility restricted to a couple of miles, and off Gravelines the sight of a French steamer piled on the beach told its own warning. In less than an hour from first starting, an explosion aft made the "Princess Maud's" people look round to find that where No. 5 lifeboat had been standing quite normally on the poop it now ceased to exist anywhere. A salvo of four shells from the French shore had wiped it away.

Captain H. Clarke therefore sheered away from the land and essayed to present a smaller sort of target but, before this alteration of course had been completed, another booming went forth and a shell pierced the waterline of the engine-room at the starboard side. Several other projectiles dropped all round the ship. Clearly she had sustained much damage, and four men were injured.

When once out of range from the Gravelines guns, "Princess Maud" again headed for Dunkirk whilst officers surveyed the harm done to vessel and First Aid to the injured was being distributed. The former was not to be lightly passed over. "The hole in the engine-room", said Captain Clarke, "proved to be a yard square and the sea was pouring in."

Mattresses were bunged in, and these eventually did prevent much of the water from percolating, yet it was hopeless to carry on in this fashion. He swung out the boats and tried every means of listing her, though it would be hopeless to keep on towards his destination. So, dodging all the wrecks and rafts, the numerous craft of all kinds that littered the Channel, Captain Clarke came back into Dover.

That was just after 4 p.m., and his men made a very fine accomplishment indeed. In theory the "Princess Maud" should have foundered whilst on passage: in practice by working hard that night and throughout the week-end, it was possible on Monday, June 3, for the ship with completed repairs to leave Dover at 8 p.m. That shows what can be accomplished when all efforts are concentrated on a big task.

She made a night crossing in a slight fog to discover Dunkirk still a marvellous spectacle ablaze, with dense clouds of smoke drifting slowly westwards, and a German battery three or four miles further westwards pumping shells into the satanic medley. Star shells were also being fired over the swept channel, in order to light up that area and hinder the "Princess Maud's" further progress.

Master mariners with wonderful unanimity deplore that swept channel which, stretching along the coast, was of only a limited width and studded with wrecks. There were so many T.B.D.'s and small craft speeding about that it made these reliable, 'safe' men attempt the most hazardous navigation. To do this repeatedly was so contrary to their pre-war custom that they did not care each time to repeat this job. If an object seemed like the wreck of a paddler, at High Water they just had to go over and hope for the best. The entrance between the jetties was even worse. Listen to Captain H. Clarke's description.

"Wrecks dotted the harbour here and there, the only light was that of shells bursting, and the occasional glare of the fires." It was bad enough to be assailed on passage, but this waiting about off the entrance till a clear berth could be ready was most trying. One had to keep clear not merely of wrecks and traffic, but of the shells which seemed to be rushing from east and west.

Midnight broke, and still "Princess Maud" tarried when an outward-bound French transport rammed her on the starboard quarter, and twelve minutes later a French trawler hit her on the port quarter and almost capsized herself. Then, at length, there would be just room for the "Princess" at the eastern jetty's extreme end, troops would clamber aboard "all ways" — no gangway being available — and even dogs, of every breed and no breed, somehow got aboard. They had come from Belgium and Holland, bereft of homes, and made friends with the kindly 'Tommies', but something had to be done about it, so these animals were shot dead.

That last night, on June 3, became unforgettable because Dunkirk was due for the blockships to be sunk early next morning. By 1-50, then, the ship being well packed with human beings she cast off ropes and made room for another. But she had barely moved away and was, in fact, just swinging when a shell went 'plonk' against the very berth she had vacated.

Coming out in the dark, she almost collided with the blockships that were waiting outside, and to make matters completely annoying "we ran into a dense fog, which in a way was a relief." Relief from what? The traffic? Well, it got so bad two hours later that the "Princess Maud" let go anchor close to the Goodwins and waited till daylight before landing her passengers.

*

Many have wondered what happened to those G.W.R. steamers which tourists in happier times patronised on their journeys from Weymouth to the Channel Isles and thence to St. Malo, or from Fishguard to Ireland. Some became transports for troops, others were with the usual Red Cross distinctive marks sent as hospital ships or carriers, though to the amazement of the civilised world the Nazi criminals paid no respect to such markings.

One conspicuous with the Red Cross notation was the company's S.S. "St. Andrew", which quite independently of the Dunkirk development was sent on May 20 from Netley to Boulogne, and although the air raids were beginning night and day on town, on quays and harbour, snatched up the wounded from a base hospital and hurried them to Southampton. Then, when Boulogne was no longer practicable, she went to Cherbourg on May 22 and fetched more patients. We have seen what happened to the "Benlawers" when she entered Calais on May 24 and emerged the next day. Hear, then, the experiences of "St. Andrew".

She was lying in the Downs and bombed when at 6 a.m., on the 24th, she made for Calais to get hold of the hospital cases. As she approached, this port looked a horrible sight — all smoke and flames — and when three cables (600 yards) off the west pierhead the shore batteries at once began straddling her. so she stood away from the entrance. An hour later she made a further effort whilst the guns again concentrated on her and paid not the slightest respect for the hospital significations and the Red Cross, which was quite plainly displayed. Perhaps too readily we had forgotten the German attacks on hospital ships in the previous war, how they had sunk the "Anglia", another "St. Andrew", and seventeen similarly marked vessels. Proof enough that whether they be known as Germans or Nazis, they are much the same under the skin.

She saw a transport working out under a withering shell-fire, then the guns were determined that "St. Andrew" should be sunk at this narrow entrance so that it might be blocked and no further attempts be made. The latter therefore once more stood off, hoping for a lull. As everyone well knows who has taken a ship into Calais, the channel is narrow and no great alteration of course is possible. When therefore she got near the transport these shore guns directed an intense fire that endangered both ships. Yet the remarkable thing was that neither received damage.

The transport got clean away, and the "St. Andrew" again approached, but the guns made it out of the question, and she returned to Dover.

Equally difficult had been the passage of her G.W.R. sister "St. Helier". This vessel had entered Calais on May 22 at Low Water and found that harbour, besides the quays, all deserted. She had come hoping to embark 2000 troops but, whilst trying to berth alongside, she was bombed by three 'planes only 1000 feet up. Some French soldiers did come out of an adjacent ruined building to help with the ropes, but matters became no easier. Since the troops did not appear, and it was a night of full moon and the bombing grew worse, she decided to clear away and get back to Dover, followed thither by the 'planes.

But these ships would be more useful at Dunkirk.

First of all on the 23rd the "St. Helier" brought 1500 British as well as French troops to Dover. Then, having bunkered, she made another attempt, but was sent back from Dunkirk and anchored in the Downs, as ships were being sunk by heavy shelling from the coast. Next time, however, she proceeded via Ostend in company with "St. Andrew" and "St. Julien". An exciting time being had by all.

The "St. Helier" was bombed, but her Master, Captain Pitman, avoided the missiles by steering for the same spot where the last had fallen and — to avoid blocking up the harbour — did not enter till the raid was over. When going alongside again, the Sea Transport Officer had to order her temporarily away; then, whilst she was waiting, the 'planes came at her, so she decided to make for Dover. But the "St. Andrew" managed to embark wounded with help from the crew, despite all the Germans' worst efforts. Captain L. T. Richardson in the "St. Julien", a hospital carrier, went right to near the Inner Locks. Fortunately the tide was low and the bombs dropped only twenty feet away, yet they gave his vessel a good shake-up. He, too, having hailed ineffectively French soldiers as to where he should berth, gave it up and returned to Dover. With seventeen 'planes sowing destruction, it was too hot for anything.

After two hours she was ordered to Dunkirk again with "St. Andrew" following, but off Calais the shells began. She embarked her cases, took them to Newhaven, but though she tried her uttermost next day could not get past the Dyck Lightship because of the land batteries, and saved herself by zigzagging.

All this meant that a heavy strain was being borne both by officers and men, and it was worse that the enemy paid no regard for our hospital ships. When on the 27th "St. Julien", followed by "St. Helier", "Kyno", and "Royal Daffodil"[4] and "St. Andrew", were met by bombs and shells near the Middlekirke buoy though escorted by two destroyers, four of them turned back. The "St. Andrew" and "St. Julien" had both been fired on by the Gravelines batteries the day previously, and seen the "Scotia"[5] attacked by one of the small German "E" torpedo craft; but the great danger on Monday the 27th was as follows.

The Sea Transport Officer warned all ships from entering because the shelling had already caused quay walls to collapse, and he feared that incoming ships might block up the harbour then and spoil all other ventures. That was why the convoy had to be re-formed and most of them sent back to the Downs. By the 29th the burden was becoming intense, but the addition to "St. Helier" of naval ratings plus twenty soldiers with Lewis guns gave Captain Pitman considerable pleasure, so that she left in a dense fog, entered Dunkirk, and embarked 2000 troops. They were making the best of things, for the weather blinded the eyes of flying craft. That day, too, the "St. Andrew" at Southampton was given concrete protection for her navigating bridge.

The "St. Julien" again proceeded, but when north of Nieuport she received a handful of flyers, and found the above-mentioned channel congested with all sorts and sizes of small craft. The same day the Isle of Man "King Orry", while trying to berth alongside Dunkirk jetty, got amid a heavy raid and was sunk. As Captain Richardson remarked, "She received her packet" in the very berth he had originally intended for himself.

Meanwhile the G.W.R. "St. David", under Captain Joy, had been doing fine things at Dunkirk, until nature took a firm hand and officers could no longer endure. First of all the Second Engineer broke down and suffered from loss of memory, then the Medical Officer was pronounced unfit for sea service, and finally on May 30, Captain Joy himself collapsed and was succeeded by the Chief Officer, Captain Mendus. It was no wonder that all this constant work, all this navigational difficulty for men proud of their job, all this nervous watching with lights out, and especially all that bombing, meant such a mighty lot. The marvel is that so many people stood things as long as they did, before giving way. Gladly Captain Richardson welcomed aboard "St. Julien" twenty naval ratings, for his splendid men were beginning to feel the burden.

As to the "St. Andrew", when she went into Dunkirk and found a whole part of the quay standing, she made the grievous discovery on June 1 that after ambulances had been bombed they were either empty on the quay, or silent with dead men. It would have been impossible to load therefrom had the sick men still been alive.

What with the tide dropping, daylight vanishing, the danger of hitting some submerged object when leaving, it was a sad moment. The enemy had well advanced, already he was on the city's outskirts and making the quays untenable. Everywhere the large fires and acrid clouds of dense smoke, confusion of shipping at the pierheads — these were the depressing environment.

The navigational buoys were too scant, the risk of overrunning the many small craft too great, the possibility of rest at the end of voyaging quite out of the question. For most of a fortnight it was a case of doubling the lookouts and forbidding men to go forward into the fo'c'sle already considered very dangerous. But, with the merest exceptions, officers and men alike carried on by a good will and untiring devotion. The nett result was that hundreds of thousands were carried from France, who otherwise would have perished on the piers.

By the last day of May the Nazis from a position five miles west of Dunkirk had the breakwaters' range and were centring an almost continuous fire. This made the handling of shipping most onerous. The "St. Helier", for example, would shoot at a 'plane by anti-aircraft fire, then resume embarking 1600 or 2000 troops but still could never be sure of getting clear in the darkness. Almost it was beyond the ken of any seafarer to avoid such mishaps.

When H.M.S. "Sharpshooter", a minesweeper of 835 tons (usually a Commander's command), came across "St. Helier's" bows and there crunched an ugly rending of steel, the warship's captain begged the other to keep steaming ahead into her at half speed with one engine so as to ease the pressure on the bulkhead. An officer of great daring told me he lost several lives and three different small craft during these ten days, but he lost likewise his voice for some time afterwards, due to the smoke and having to shout among that din.

The services of a tug eventually helped "Sharpshooter", but then, whilst still manoeuvring, the "Princess Eleanora" crashed into the "St. Helier's" starboard bows, and the latter could not avoid driving right over a wreck though she brought her passengers safely to Dover. Captain Pitman even in daylight was being tried by all possible circumstances. He hoped on June 1 to dash in at 3-30 p.m., embark the soldiers and rush out again, when suddenly he was asked to wait another 2½ hours longer for a load of stretcher cases on their way.

He was therefore shifting berth when a couple of shells smote his docking-bridge and slightly wounded the Second Mate. The exciting interlude lengthened, bombardment was continued, and seven hours passed ere he could get away. Even then his Chief Officer, Mr H. D. Freeman, with the Second Officer, Mr F. Martin, had to come ashore and help in carrying the wounded from Dunkirk jetty to the ship.

But why single out these Deck Officers when everybody was doing his very best? The Engineers told the Captain "as long as the vessel remains afloat" they were prepared to do whatever might be required. And they kept their word.

After landing his troops in England that Sunday morning, the Naval Authorities came to Captain Pitman and considered that he had done enough. They were prepared to put in his place a Naval Commander. But the "old man" would not hear of the suggestion: he was going to see the job through to the finish. Let the naval officer and his ten ratings come and help take off troops from the beaches, but he for his own part would stick to his captaincy.

It was this magnificent example of persistent energy and courage that helped to keep things going at such a critical period. Only a few more days remained ere it would be too late, and the enemy in possession of those piers. So he went across, loaded 2000 more of the B.E.F. and even stood by for yet another trip, but luckily no longer this became necessary. Moreover the ship had recently become difficult to handle, especially at the quays, when examination proved that because of the collisions and underwater explosions her forepeak was full of water.

So, when the war is all over and the unthinking tourist makes a trip in "St. Helier" again, let it be remembered that she made one venturous voyage towards Calais and back, besides seven to Dunkirk.

Nor can we omit that tragic ultimate episode of the S.S. "Paris" equally known to thousands of people that have crossed the Channel in her on the way to France. We mentioned just now the tug "Foremost 87" which, after her visit to Calais, had been lying in Dover harbour. On Sunday afternoon, June 2, the latter was ordered to take the R.N.L.I. life-boats "Cecil and Lillian Philpott" and the "Thomas Kirk Wright" part of the way towards Dunkirk.

She did this towing all right, arrived at the chosen spot, was just giving the commanders their courses towards Dunkirk harbour when Captain Fryer noticed something wrong to the southward. The hospital ship "Paris" (1790 tons) of Newhaven certainly was in difficulties, and as he approached her he perceived several boats full of survivors but still being bombed and machine-gunned, whereupon he ordered his crew to get life-lines ready.

It was a ghastly sight that so able a vessel should have been mercilessly sunk by inhumane monsters of the sky taking no heed of her character. It was blackguardly that some of the very seriously injured were Nursing Sisters, that others were the scalded victims of the engine-room. But by this time one knew that Nazis had forfeited all sense of decency. The tug managed to pick up 95 survivors, one of whom died aboard, but the rest being made as comfortable as possible, he headed for Dover and brought them to safety with the utmost despatch.

CHAPTER XIV — HOW THE SHIPS TRIUMPHED

DURING the entire night of May 29-30 it seemed part of the enemy's plan to give such a terrific bombardment to Dunkirk by air and land as to make the place impossible for steamers as a port of call. Town and quays received a tremendous hammering for the one purpose of preventing our Army from being taken away, and the result was that the place was fast getting into that condition which filled naval officers and experienced mariners with serious forebodings.

Still, these soldiers had to be taken out of France and the ships alone could do it. Each trip became more difficult than the last. The "St. David" under her new Master, Captain Mendus, went boldly at the effort on May 31, found the place more littered than ever with wrecks, and those underwater explosions against the hull quite alarming.

Today she was signalled off Dunkirk not to enter just yet, so that whilst standing off-and-on outside he had to bear patiently seven separate aerial attacks during which once a magnetic mine fell so close ahead that he only saved the ship by going full speed astern with his engines. Twenty minutes later another mine blew up a hundred feet away, and yet another magnetic ambush dropped a mere four feet from the starboard quarter.

Backing out of the harbour at night after the town had been pulverised by field guns, and with the ship lit up by parachute flares to help bombers and distant artillery, did not make the new skipper's life any more pleasant. His efforts to enter Dunkirk on Saturday, June 1, were not practicable and even on the return passage till anchored off Dover there seemed no respite, since a terrible explosion happened twenty yards from his port quarter. The enemy had followed him all the way across.

This time, the port machinery and shaft became badly damaged, and the compasses in the ship rendered useless. Captain Mendus was therefore sent for repairs to Southampton, which seems quite easy enough. Unfortunately trouble does not come singly, so what with no reliable compass and the Channel that day being thick with haze, the "St. David" spent quite a long and anxious time on the journey.

The only G.W.R. vessel which had not been degaussed for this purpose was the S.S. "Roebuck", which went to La Panne and fetched 500 men, but she was very soon put back on the regular sailing list to Guernsey, from June 6, though we know that these voyagings terminated shortly afterwards.

Whilst Skippers understood very well why their services were needed so much and why their ships were lying in the Downs, always there was an element of uncertainty as to what would next befall them. Take for instance the S.S. "Nephrite", owned by Stephenson Clarke & Associated Companies of London. Her Master, Captain C. G. West, was the kind of man who gets things done and whom a crew loves as a leader.

She was lying off Deal when orders came to her via the Examination Tug at 6 a.m. of May 31 that she was to proceed for Dunkirk. She had been originally loaded with military stores, and German 'planes this last night had been patrolling the Downs. It was good, therefore, to be up and doing. All hands were put on to stripping cases, drums of oil got rid of, drinking water obtained, and the cargo in the holds so levelled down that space for troops was found and they reckoned she would stow 900 men.

So "Nephrite" got under way at once through the Downs in fine, clear weather. Food from the cargo was being prepared ahead for guests, and the galley kept busy. It was before ten that morning the Nazi 'planes, like seagulls, foretold approach to the Belgian coast hiding itself beneath the pall of smoke. Sounds of firing and bombs dropping grew more intense, ships homeward-bound full of khaki passed, and soon "Nephrite" entered the narrow channel that led to Dunkirk.

The wrecks showed up, our own aircraft were on the enemy's tails above, the harbour entrance seemed as congested as other mariners had hinted; but a berth was soon found alongside, *zoo* soldiers were glad to troop aboard and dine off the cooked food. Among the several officers one was a Padre and one a Jewish doctor. To them Captain West gave up the use of his cabin, whilst the steward continuously was employed getting more meals ready. Eat? These visitors had partaken of but one meal in the last three days.

"I'm sorry", apologised the host, "but there's pork in this stew."

The Doctor was not in the least worried. He felt mad with hunger, and the odour enticed him. Said he,

"I do not mind if there are dead dogs in it. I am going to have my share: it smells so good."

Of course the meal had to be interrupted when "Nephrite" was ordered to shift alongside the "Roebuck" to avoid taking the ground at Low Water, as the former drew over 14 feet. There was plenty to occupy the mind because of destroyers, hospital ships, and trawlers perpetually on the move or embarking troops; the harassed Commander R.N. directing from the pier; and the bombers swooping from the clouds. But one of the crew, Mellis, seemed continually in action with his Lewis gun, and willing aid from the soldiers was quickly forthcoming.

The destroyers hit back with all their guns, shells from the land whined and flopped into the harbour. So it went on till six that evening. The pier was crowded with French troops who, though eager to come and dine, did not relish travelling to a British port; so, after consultation with a French Major, Captain West decided that having 500 soldiers — 430 British and 70 *poilus* — he should cast off and steam out of the harbour.

On the way home Captain West organised a party of ten soldiers on the fo'c'sle head, to fire at any craft that should come within range. This suited Mellis excellently, who put in some great work with his gun, registering hits on three enemy 'planes and bringing two down. Really it was a happy voyage, because of a happy skipper. The men had all forfeited their berths and grub to the soldiers, and there was a bit of sport against 'Jerry'. So, when at dusk Captain West sighted the North Goodwin Light Vessel and presently let go anchor off Deal till daybreak, most of the troops slept so soundly that the nocturnal visit of a Nazi aeroplane could not wake them.

The bursting next morning of a magnetic mine close to the fairway leading into Folkestone harbour was nothing, but what did impress Captain West was that all these warriors immediately washed and shaved before landing.

It was a pity that all the crossings could not be so pleasant, or that much needed slumber was so barely disturbed. When Captain R. Hughes took the S.S. "Killarney", owned by the Coast Lines, across one night in May from the Downs past Calais to Dunkirk he found many things to cause trepidation. The misty weather obliterated all navigational aids, and from dawn the usual dumps were belching forth the heavy smoke.

But whilst awaiting her turn to enter and pick up troops, the "Killarney" had another ship in company. Quick as lightning a violent explosion burst, the centre of that neighbouring ship disappeared in a cloud of smoke and when the cloud lazily rolled away it revealed only bits and pieces. For the stern portion from mainmast aft had vanished, then two minutes later the forward part heeled over and sank.

It was thus that the "Mona's Queen" disappeared on a magnetic mine.

An hour later, somewhat upset by this fiendish wickedness, the "Killarney" went alongside the breakwater and embarked troops of all regiments, some being stretcher cases which faithful chums had carried through four days and four nights. As the ship sped forth out of the harbour, down the Roads and past Gravelines, utterly wearied soldiers stretched out all over the ship were snatching the first decent rest after their retreating.

Bang! Bang! Bang!

Three German shore batteries mounting 5.9-inch guns decided to interrupt. The first shell dropped into the water just short of the port wing by the bridge. Immediately Captain Hughes placed his ship stern on to the shore, increased speed and began zigzagging, whilst the engineers rendered first-class help by belching out a screen of smoke. But it was tricky going, beyond the swept channel, over the sandbanks.

Shells so rapidly succeeded each other that within forty minutes 90 were fired. Unfortunately one missile struck the after end of the boat-deck and fell amongst a group of men, killing eight and wounding thirty. Luckily there was an R.A.M.C. doctor travelling, and he rendered with the "Killarney's" medicine chest what help could be given for dressing gunshot wounds.

Fifteen minutes later appeared a machine-gunning aircraft, but one of our Spitfires flew out of the clouds and with a burst against the German's tail sent it crashing down to fall six hundred yards away into the sea on the port side. Three of our bombers then flew out to escort "Killarney", but they indicated her to alter course. What now?

The ship did as bidden, and sure enough she soon sighted the reason. There, ahead, was a raft bearing one French officer and two Belgian soldiers. It proved to be a very flimsy affair fashioned out of some old wood and a door, yet those three men were optimists who deserved better fortune, and evidently hoped to hit the French coast. They had brought with them two tins of biscuits, six demi-johns of wine and (ridiculous to state) a very ancient bicycle carefully lashed down.

There was not much time to be wasted under the circumstances, the men were picked up but the British crew found no little difficulty in convincing the wanderers that at least the bicycle could not be accommodated. So when the dead and wounded, the fit Englishmen and recovered French were landed at Dover, Captain Hughes decided to call it a day.

Thus every voyage to Dunkirk was different. A ship might come one route or another, she might be fortunate or death-pursued. Nothing was regular other than the persistent onslaughts, and these by their sudden ways none could guarantee for occurrence except that off the pier heads was generally a likely spot.

You may be quite sure that our seafarers were always ready to put up a good fight, and at least they had the advantage of seeing the enemy with their own eyes. In the last war little better than a periscope was visible — oftentimes not even that. But it gave no little satisfaction to fisherman or sailor that to-day he could get his own back and do something for his ship and pals by bringing to earth a Nazi flying craft.

There was the S.S. "Levenwood", owned in Middlesbrough, lying a couple of miles east of Dunkirk on the last day of May. Her Master, Captain W. O. Young, was well aware that she was only an 803 tons ship, that the North Sea was an unhealthy place, but he had a 12-pdr., also a Lewis gun, and a Bren. What was more, in Mr. G. Knight he had a splendid Merchant Navy gunner, with a clear eye and steady aim; for it is remarkable that such men are born shots and the very match for marauders. With his first shell from the 12-pdr. the latter brought down a Nazi enemy, which went crashing on to the dunes. Therefore, with him at the big weapon, and Chief Officer working a Lewis gun, they were able to make the "Levenwood" unpleasant enough.

But at Dunkirk — in the early days at least — there was, as we have observed, a great shortage of wherries and small boats such as could be sent to the beaches and come off to the anchored shipping: in fact it had been proved the day previously that it took about five or six hours to bring from 1000 to 1200 troops from shore to offlying destroyer. Considering the race against time, the inevitability of Germans entering the port soon, and the thousands of Allies yet to be withdrawn, this rate was altogether too slow.

An officer suggested to Captain Young that the "Levenwood" be put on the beach and then send her ship's lifeboats to facilitate the embarkation. So the forepeak tank was blown and the ship placed her nose on the shelving beach in about 8 feet of water, whilst the Captain kept steaming slow ahead all the while to prevent the ship swinging broadside on with the rising tide. Thus by simple seamanship he managed to keep the vessel about a quarter of a mile from where the beach dried out.

At the same time he lowered his boats, these were drawn to and from the beach by a clever arrangement of ropes, and thus plenty of soldiers were helped aboard. This went on with the utmost difficulty because 'Jerry' from topside tried amusing himself with bombs whilst an ugly surf driving shorewards made any boathandling awkward. As the tide rose, it was becoming more and more impossible to hold the vessel in position, but soldiers waist deep and more waded out to the boats.

It persisted for three hours — from 2-30 p.m. till 5-50 — when one of the boats was badly holed and "Levenwood" had to come off at High Water. The Captain encouraged his people to make one last trip to the beach, despite the rising surf, and in so doing a boat was swamped. Both the British and French troops were very good and disciplined, there was no sort of panic, so they were all saved after being thrown into the sea although still mighty weary.

It is a great pleasure to record how well everybody helped each other, and no one deemed himself superfluous. Forty bombers might do their damnedest but Mr. R. Moodey, one of the ship's firemen, continued diving overboard and swimming to the soldiers. Like a father he kept alive the drooping spirits of troops almost too tired for further contending. He swam back with them who otherwise might have given up, he persuaded some unable to swim through the breaking waves, and for three suspenseful hours he was battering with the heavy swell till finally the last soldier had been put aboard, the "Levenwood" got herself well afloat and steamed on towards England.

But many were the other instances of real heroism that will never find record. Some have been too self-effacing, others have perished in the attempt, yet the troops know well in their private memories how deep is their gratitude towards men willing to lay down precious lives.

CHAPTER XV — HELL'S DELIGHT

THIS matter of the Dunkirk withdrawal completely upset the arrangements which were still being made for other matters such as landing supplies for the troops. Ships had to be switched off towards more immediate tasks.

That fine vessel "Clan Macalister" of the Clan Line, owned by Messrs. Cayzer, Irvine & Co., after she reached Southampton was sent to the Downs and left the latter at 3-30 a.m. of May 29, making towards the dunes of Bray several miles east of Dunkirk. From the first, Captain R. W. Mackie appreciated this would be no pleasant excursion as he passed through the Downs and avoided one of the wrecks which cluttered up the West Goodwins. Twelve hours later he found an air-raid off Bray dominating the roadstead, but on looking aft he further discovered aerial damage to his No. 5 hold and the gun-platform. To cut this story short, the "Clan Macalister" was alight, beams and other parts of the hatch twisted, a large hole on deck, and the crew's quarters just a mass of twisted woodwork. Moreover the bomb penetrating through the side further aft had so burst that dead were lying about the decks. This had happened with startling suddenness.

Seeing her plight, H.M.S. "Malcolm", a 1530-tons flotilla leader, steamed alongside the burning ship to take off soldiers and injured crew, but it was not easy. Two lines of hose were passed aboard and directed at No. 5 hold, but could not reach the gun-platform already well alight. The "Clan Macalister's" own hose failed because the deck-service pipe had been broken and in places holed, so there existed too little pressure.

There remained to be dumped overboard a certain amount of ammunition and petrol, when the aeroplanes issued forth more alarmingly, so "Malcolm" had to cast off. The "Clan Macalister" continued at slow speed, her hose doing its best from aft, but all too certainly the conflagration gained. The rifle ammunition every few minutes kept popping off and made it too dangerous for approach. But at least Captain Mackie knew that his engines were working ahead all right, his shafting undamaged, and his steering gear in good trim.

Yet no sooner had he started again than the wretched aeroplanes sped out, and one bomb just missed the fore end of the bridge by the port side. It stopped the gyro compass, it shook the ship badly from stem to stern, and the telemotor was broken. Things looked critical.

Explaining the position to the Engineers, the Captain emphasised that no one could stay aft and steer: the blazing fires and danger from the spare ammunition might any moment be fatal. And just as he himself was about to look further astern, the first of the big shells exploded. So the plain statement of affairs meant that the ship was "for it". She could not get out seaward, she could not steer through the encircling sandbanks: clearly she seemed marked out for final destruction. So what?

The Captain made a signal to a destroyer, which was inshore engaged taking troops aboard.

"We want assistance here."

But the stranger could not have seen the morse, and failed to answer.

At that time a 710 tons minesweeper, H.M.S. "Pangbourne", entering the roads, did perceive the ship in distress and with true naval gallantry came alongside with his twin screw.

"My telemotor is broken, and I cannot get clear."

"All right! We'll take you on board —"

The "Clan Macalister's" Chief and 5th Engineers had been below and drawn the fires to the best of their ability. The crew were mustered, and only 12 Europeans plus 23 natives were numbered. Then it was time to leave her.

Sad for a Captain to make that awful decision concerning a vessel he loved so well, but she was burning fiercely aft. The "Pangbourne" bore them shorewards, but being so frequently raided and having lost many lives, the ship also herself holed, she resolved to go homewards.

On the way matters were not peaceful, for they fell in with the "Gracie Fields" which also was carrying troops. A bomb having struck her, she was in a pretty plight and longed for a tow. The "Pangbourne" obliged and did so for several hours, but the time came when she began sinking lower and lower till at last her people likewise were transferred and she must be abandoned. Narrowly the minesweeper escaped a magnetic mine off the South Goodwin Light Vessel, but with all her rescuees she steamed safely into Dover.

It will be remembered by many that years ago, at the blocking of Zeebrugge on St. George's Day, 1918, two ex-Liverpool ferry steamers known as the "Daffodil" and "Iris" were employed to assist H.M.S. "Vindictive". Later on these ships were allowed, on returning to civil life, to prefix the title "Royal". The time came likewise for a new ship to be built as "Royal Daffodil", managed by the General Steam Navigation Company, and this vessel with an honoured name played her part in the Second German War.

Of 2060 tons, the "Royal Daffodil" was able to fetch most of 9000 troops from France between May 27 and the day when "Paris" was sunk. It is true that five aerial torpedoes were dropped on the "Royal Daffodil", that they all missed, but the sixth passing through three decks entered the engine-room and went through the starboard side. Even then it exploded clear of the vessel, but the missile's collar went through the bilge.

Now the engines having been stopped, the "Royal Daffodil" was machine-gunned with tracer bullets by the aircraft, starting small fires. She also began to leak through a hole made by the bomb, and was listed to starboard. To counteract this, gear was shifted to her port side, the boats lowered to deck level and filled with water, this resulting in raising the starboard side sufficiently to lift the hole just clear of her waterline. The Chief Engineer, Mr J. W. Coulthard, and his Second then took all beds they could lay their hands upon and plugged the hole.

It was an extremely able attempt, for the Second Engineer stood up to his neck in the water holding open the bilge valve whilst the Senior kept the pump going. This being a Diesel engine, there was a great risk. She got back and landed all on board.

But the following report, written by her Master, Captain G. Johnson, speaks for itself.

"At 6.30 a.m. on the 27th May, we left Dover under escort bound for Dunkirk. On approaching the French Coast, our escort ordered us to return to the Downs, owing to Enemy shelling and air activity on the route. On arrival at the Downs, we were ordered to Dunkirk via the route which took you over past the West Hinder and Middlekerke Buoys. Five Vessels left together. A very heavy air raid was in progress when we arrived off Dunkirk and we were attacked outside of the harbour. I decided to enter, having chosen the inner West Pier; the other vessels having turned back. Whilst mooring, a bomb dropped between the bow and the Quay, demolishing part of the Quay. Other bombs dropped in close proximity to the vessel. After lying alongside for 10 minutes the air cleared, ambulances drove down the Quay and the crew assisted in getting on board, in addition to the walking wounded, 40 stretcher cases. All troops that were available were taken before being ordered out. An approximate total for that day being 950. These troops were taken to Dover, and after being disembarked, the vessel was anchored at 1 a.m. on the 28th inst.

"At 5.30 p.m. on the 28th we left Dover for Dunkirk, but on arrival found it impossible to approach the berth used on our previous voyage. I swung the vessel and moored to the Eastern Breakwater. Raids were in progress but no direct attack was being delivered on the harbour. Visibility was bad owing to the intense smoke from shore tanks and one ship which were on fire. There was a breach in this breakwater, and on instructions the Chief Officer, Mr. A. Paterson, left the ship's gangways to help to fill in this gap. We left each voyage from the Port on the instructions of the R.N. Commander in charge. The number we evacuated on this trip we estimate to be in the region of 1800 men. We returned to Margate.

"At 8.30 a.m. on the 29th May we left Margate for Dunkirk. No undue incident occurred on our outward passage. On our return journey, having embarked 1700 troops, heavy shelling was experienced from the shore battery at Nieuport, shells falling over and short of us and the range was being found. At this period one of H.M. Destroyers, after overtaking us, laid an efficient smoke screen which undoubtedly saved the ship. We returned to Dover, arriving there the same evening.

"At 7.45 p.m. on the 30th May we left Dover with orders to proceed to La Panne beach, arriving there during very poor visibility caused by smoke and mist on the coast. We cruised about for three hours, during which time shore batteries were very active. After grounding and being unable to attract attention, we were obliged to return to Margate, arriving 5.10 a.m. on the 31st and anchoring in the roadstead.

"At 4 p.m. on the 31st May, we left Margate and returned to Dover with 2500 French Troops. This voyage was without undue incident.

"On June 1st at 3 p.m. we left Dover by a new route, which was between minefields, taking us over towards the Ruytingen Bank, West of Dunkirk. On nearing the French coast we were met by M.V. "Royal

Sovereign" and a French Destroyer who ordered us to return owing to heavy fire from shore batteries at Gravelines. We returned to Margate.

"At 10 p.m. the same night we left Margate via the above-mentioned route. I experienced great difficulty when approaching Dunkirk owing to uncharted wrecks and smoke, eventually berthing well inside of the Western Breakwater, having found the outer end breached in two places. We embarked 1900 British and French Troops, returning to Margate a.m. the 2nd.

"On the evening of this day, the 2nd inst., it was arranged that the Troopships and Destroyers should proceed to Dunkirk at 20 minute intervals. This vessel to be the first to proceed, we left at 5.30 p.m. so as to arrive at Dunkirk at 9 p.m. At 7.50 p.m. six Enemy bombers attacked us with bombs and machine-gun fire, scoring one hit with a delayed action bomb which holed the ship's side at the waterline, exploding clear of the stern. The machine-gun attack caused one fatality and 2 casualties. An efficient barrage was put up by the ship's machine-guns, otherwise, without doubt, the vessel would have been more successfully bombed. The four-inch gun on this ship is not H.A.

"Several bombs dropped close to us, the concussion of one causing switches to jump out at the main switchboard, which made the engines temporarily stop. We were then 17.5 miles S.E. by E, from the North Goodwin Lightvessel. Before the commencement of this trip a R.N. Commander with Ratings boarded to assist with the embarkation. The Commander came to me and said we had been holed.

"I at first thought, from my position on the bridge, the bomb had missed, seeing a large volume of water under the stem with the subsequent heavy explosion. The Chief Officer came to the bridge and informed me the damage was below the waterline on the starboard side, I then gave orders to have all movable gear shifted to port. I then left the bridge and came to the saloon deck where I met the Chief Engineer, who informed me that water was making in the engine-room. I told him what measures were being taken to try and stop it, and he said he could also help by transferring the Fuel Oil from the starboard tank to the port tank. Beds were jammed into the hole and tommied down. Hoses in the port life-boats, already swung out, also helped to give the ship a further list. The vessel was stopped for about 10 minutes, during which time she was driving to the northward with the N.E., Spring Tide. The Chief Engineer informed me that he could now move the engines, so we proceeded at about half speed.

"After going at this speed for some time, the Chief Engineer stated that he must reduce speed as water had entered the oil system. I had, during this time, refused the assistance of two of Alexander's tugs, as I saw the Hospital ship "Paris" had been bombed and was sinking, and I told them to go to her assistance, knowing we could take to the boats in ample time if required. I found on approaching the North Goodwin Lightvessel that we were driving fast to the Northward, which area was mined. I asked the Chief Engineer if he could increase the speed, and he said, now that they had got the water from the sump he could do so.

"We arrived off Ramsgate at 10.30 p.m. where a tug was sent to take off casualties and R.N. Ratings. I could not remain close to the Harbour entrance on a falling tide, therefore, after the tug left I decided to drop up to a safer anchorage, the Chief Engineer stated he could manage this. I dredged into 3½ fathoms and brought up. A signal was sent to me stating that The Admiralty Salvage Officer would come to us later. The Chief Engineer told me it would be impossible to move the engines further.

"I informed the Salvage Officer of this fact on his arrival on board at 3.15 p.m. on the 3rd inst., and it was decided to tow to Dover. This was started at 5 a.m. the same day, by salvage vessel "Forde" and tug "Doria". We anchored off Dover at 7 a.m. and entered that port at 2.30 p.m. berthing at the South Arm. The following day, the 4th inst., the vessel was berthed in the Wellington Dock for temporary patching.

"As regards the exact number of Troops carried, difficulty was experienced, in obtaining an exact check owing to so many men boarding over rails and ladders. Our estimated total was 8850, although a shore official told me the number was greater; this I doubt."

It is a pleasure to be able to add that among the awards afterwards made in connection with the Dunkirk deeds, both the name of Mr A. Paterson, Chief Officer, and of Mr J. W. Coulthard, Chief Engineer, were given as receiving the D.S.C. aboard the "Royal Daffodil". The ship had now in this Second War obtained a fresh fame.

The reader will notice that Captain Johnson makes mention of the General Steam Navigation Company's ship "Royal Sovereign". I have therefore thought it well to add the report of the latter's Master, Captain T. J. Aldis. The Chief Engineer, Mr A. Sinclair, of the "Royal

Sovereign", also won the D.S.C. That Captain Aldis managed to make no fewer than 7 voyages and carried at least 11,000 troops on six voyages from Dunkirk is an amazing record. The times are written clockwise — 2340 signifying 11-40 p.m., 0250 meaning 2-50 a.m., and so on.

"*May 26th* whilst laying in Southampton Roads received orders to get ready to proceed at two hours' notice.

"*May 27th* at 1320 received orders to proceed to Dover and at 1500 hove up and proceeded on passage. 2340 passed through Folkestone gateway.

"*May 28th* 0020 received visual signals from Dover to anchor in Downs. 1150 saw first raid carried out on shipping, but raider successfully driven off. 1740 received orders to sail at 2030 for Dunkirk, using prescribed route.

"*May 29th* 0250 arrived off East Jetty Dunkirk and anchored, whole west side of town in flames. 0445 hove up and proceeded to Eastern Jetty. 0455 in berth and commenced embarking troops. 0535 ship filled with troops, each man having been given a lifebelt and received instruction on same. 0540 Clear of harbour. 0858 reported floating mine to patrol vessel. 0925 stopped by examination vessel and ordered to Margate Pier. 1010 anchored off Pier. 1215 arrived alongside Pier, x 330 left Margate Pier. 1735 arrived off La Panne and witnessed a heavy dive-bombing attack carried out with heavy losses to shipping. 1800, hove up anchor and proceeded to assist m.v. "Bullfinch"[6] laden with troops and ashore. 1815 "Bullfinch" afloat and proceeded. 1820 commenced embarking troops from beaches.

"*May 30th* 0410, hove up and proceeded lower down beach. 0430 embarking more troops. 05 30 vessel full, and proceeded to Margate. 1023, arrived off Margate. 1135 alongside of Margate Pier disembarking troops. 1300 left Margate. 1735 anchored off Dunkirk on naval instructions. 1820 anchored and commenced embarking troops.

"*May 31st* 0130 hove up and proceeded. 0315 stopped at Dyck buoy to pick up four survivors of a French steamer, which had been bombed. 0710 arrived alongside Margate Pier. 0830 anchored off Pier. 1803, hove up and proceeded towards Dunkirk. 2210 anchored off Pontoon Pier at Dunkirk. 2240 ordered by H.M. ship to La Panne, hove up and proceeded. 2315 anchored off La Panne.

"*June 1st*. 0220, troops on board, terrific bombarding and shelling of beach taking place so hove up and proceeded. 0615, anchored off Margate Roads. 0745, hove up and proceeded to Pier. 0830 at anchor under 1 hour's notice. 1315, left for Dunkirk. 1320, attacked and bombed by enemy aircraft, three bombs dropped; avoiding action taken. 1352, attacked and bombed by aircraft three bombs being dropped, again took avoiding action, and by doing so definitely saved ship. Now came under heavy fire from enemy position at Gravelines Pier, and as two ships appeared to be blocking channel returned to Margate for instructions. 1730, arrived Margate Roads. 1900 vessel under 1 hour's notice.

"*June 2nd* 0115 received orders to sail. 0140 received orders not to sail. 1800 left anchorage. 2000 passed Hospital ship 'Paris', having been bombed and ship's company in lifeboats, but all very cheerful and proceeded to Dunkirk. 2100 Heavy firing from shore batteries. 2130 arrived at Dunkirk and commenced embarking French troops from middle pier in harbour. 2205 cleared harbour with more than complement of troops.

"*Monday, June 3rd*. 0155 arrived at Margate Pier and commenced disembarking troops. 0203, anchored off Pier. 1200 returned to Pier. 1400, four seamen and two catering staff leave ship. 2015 left for Dunkirk. 2055, dense fog, visibility reduced to nil, but continue towards Dunkirk.

"*Tuesday, June 4th*. 0115, had slight collision with unknown steamer off No. 3 Dunkirk buoy. 0220 arrived at middle pier in harbour. 0255, overladen with troops and left pier, cutting our own forward ropes. Heavy gun-fire continuously; leaving harbour saw crew of unknown vessel being rescued by small boats. 0600, arrived Margate after 1 hour's dense fog, and disembarked troops and at 0700 departed to anchorage. 2000 hove up and proceeded to Southampton. 2355 'Royal Sovereign' lightvessel abeam.

"*June 5th* 0925, anchored at Netley."

CHAPTER XVI — THE TUGS GO TO IT

ON earlier pages we have seen something of the work done by those busy tugs of the River Thames, their multifarious duties, their collecting of craft from river to the Downs and Dover. We have in the course of our inquiry considered them rather as adjuncts to other vessels, but it will now be our duty to consider Dunkirk's operations strictly from the tugmaster's own angle. For there is no seamanship in the world of a higher class, none more delicate than when compelled to do their customary work among the Thames confines: but the purely abnormal duties of navigating craft to the French coast under the hardest conditions are such as will long be remembered with respect by all who went down to those shores in sail, steam, or motor.

We saw just now the tug "Cervia" in a light wind leaving Dover at 9-45 p.m. on May 31 for Malo, whose beach lies to the eastward of Dunkirk. She was towing the sailing barge "Royalty", but was in company of the tug "Persia", which towed a couple of barges. So many were the destroyers in the Downs, so pitch black the darkness, that Captain W. H. Simmons, Master of the "Cervia", kept his navigation lights burning. Indeed, notwithstanding the gentle air ruffling the sea, the stern barge of "Persia's" tow twice broke adrift because of the heavy swell which these destroyers in passing produced.

There were curious incidents to be met with those days, and all sorts of vessels coming out in a hurry from West Dunkirk roadstead loaded with troops; but one with twenty Belgian motor fishermen had left it rather late. Here in the early days of Saturday morning, June 1, the foreigner bore down to ask the way to England!

"I sang out the course," said Captain Simmons, "told him to follow the other traffic and he would be all right. Afterwards I learned that they passed over the Goodwin Sands at High Water and landed their troops and refugees in our country."

Sailors repeatedly have mentioned to me the procession of fast destroyers and 21-knots cross-Channel steamers which, like express trains, seemed to make the sea one dangerous traffic route, and the

"Cervia" many times had to ease down till they passed. Then as she observed Dunkirk's pierheads, the destroyers were backing out with their embarkation loads in a furious hurry to maintain their schedule. It was all such a wild night under nature's own peaceable conditions.

At last the "Cervia" slipped her tow one mile east of the jetty and at 7-20 a.m. steered well inshore of Malo, dropping anchor out of the way. Soldiers commenced running down to the "Royalty", the guns were banging away on the port's approaches, the air raid siren then blew its shrill warning and the soldiers rushed back to shelter.

But a British destroyer fired at the enemy 'planes, whose bombs kept falling dangerously near, as she steamed about at full speed with her helm hard aport. Nine of these missiles dropped in a line to the water close to the destroyer's side, and exploded with such an effect that the warship heeled well over to her beam ends, then righted herself almost as quickly. One of H.M. Sloops came along to help with her gun-fire, drove the Nazis away, whilst the latter rattled machine-gun fire against the "Cervia", who returned the assault by the power of her Lewis gun.

It was too intimately unpleasant a spot, and "Cervia" deemed it best to weigh anchor, to keep moving rather than be sunk through direct overhead hits or run down by the destroyers that twisted and turned in all directions. Captain Simmons could see the crew and soldiers of one sailing barge rowing in their boat, so picked them up and those of the barge "Duchess" which had come to anchor.

The next wave of bombers flew out of the sky, and the destroyer looked odd: she was pouring out steam and smoke, beginning to take an ugly list. To her aid the "Cervia" and the tug "St. Abbs" began steaming, but the 'planes were so determined to finish off the destroyer that the two tugs could do nothing except sheer off. It made a horrible sight whilst the guns of the destroyer all the time kept barking and she steamed round and round. Then she stopped. The enemy had registered another accurate hit.

What then?

The only chance was for the destroyer to let go anchor, swing to the tide, and it was time to abandon ship. She was H.M.S. "Keith". The crew were taking to boats and rafts, and again "Cervia" did her best to get near, but once more the enemy swooped low and was spluttering bullets as the seamen were leaping overboard. The tugs all the same could not leave the scene, and one named the "Vincia", approaching from the east end of the roadstead, began picking up survivors whilst the "St. Abbs" went alongside the destroyer's bow, and the "Cervia" was able to pick up a motorboat full of soldiers.

Meanwhile Captain Simmons could discern that another destroyer had become disabled west of the harbour, and a 'plane had dropped her bomb on a small oil-tanker astern of the "Vincia". The tanker went up in flames, a direct hit got the destroyer. She sank to the bottom.

Barely had "Cervia" noted this awful picture, than she sighted a signal summoning her to "Tollesbury" and, on going alongside this barge with the 200 men below hatches, fortunately it was possible to tow her out of the raging fury. Still more wonderful, the "Persia" succeeded in getting a line on to a destroyer. This was H.M.S. "Ivanhoe", 1370 tons, and she stuck to her manfully.

Imagine, then, that amazing display of three tugs through the roadstead. There was "Cervia" hauling the barge, the "Vincia" with her decks laden with survivors from the first destroyer, and the "Persia" towing "Ivanhoe", who could still work one engine. The moment arrived when they all drew nigh to that buoy, around which they must turn towards the open sea, but the Germans knew all about this 'windy corner'.

The enemy's shore batteries were concentrating with ardour, twenty of his aircraft flew towards the cavalcade, but "Ivanhoe" put up a splendid smoke screen. Nine bombs were seen to fall yet they were alongside an inward-bound cross-Channel steamer, so the tugs still kept going.

Fritz and Hans nevertheless did not give up their attempts immediately, since five bombs dropped so near to "Cervia" that they were 100 feet from the port bow and lifted her hull bodily out of the water. Another, aimed at the "Persia", just missed though it splashed the latter's deck, whilst yet another barely avoided the "Vincia".

However, the procession gradually by pluck and luck got clear of the inferno, and the "Persia" had the satisfaction of bringing "Ivanhoe" back to the Thames estuary, whence it would be possible for repairs to be made at Chatham; the "Vincia" got free, and the "Cervia" reached England with 230 khaki men plus the barge "Tollesbury" and crew, plus the crews of "Duchess" and "Royalty", together with the motorboat "Orient IV".

That June 1 will not be quickly forgotten by the Thames tug men. Their help was demanded everywhere this day around the Dunkirk region, doing the most desperate jobs, and it was difficult to settle whether His Majesty's Navy depended more on the Merchant Navy, or vice versa. If only something could have been done about those Nazis with their bombs and guns, if only we had been strong enough aloft to drive the Germans out of the sky, things would have been entirely different and every one of the ships permitted to get on with her particular duties. It was barely possible at once to assist the soldiers and protect the vessels from being wiped off the effective list instantly.

There were so many items for the tugs to bear in mind, so many distressed mariners to be saved. After the steam tug "Tanga" on May 31 brought in seven hours to Dunkirk the very much wanted half a dozen boats to the beaches, there to be filled with troops, she was met with the usual aerial hatred. It was while "Tanga" was abreast Dunkirk on June 1 that she sighted a small boat containing six men. They were the sole survivors of H.M. Tug "St. Fagan" which had been bombed, and two of her three Thames barges.

One mile further on the "Tanga" picked up the barge "Pudge", as stated on another page, with four men aboard (two badly wounded) and towed her back to Ramsgate. It was on June 2 the "Tanga" also rescued 90 British and 80 French troops from the burning port, when she had to clear out and make a run for it. Next day she tried again, and on the 4th she had the satisfaction of bringing down a 'plane, but yet those French refugees bound for England in any craft obtainable still continued. As an example, when three miles from the North Goodwin the "Tanga" fell in with a French lugger. She carried a crew of three, did not know where they were, so the tug took charge and anchored them off Ramsgate.

Really it seems beyond all contemplation that these fine little steam and motor vessels could ever have been dispensed with. Listen to four days' work of the "Kenia" patrolling her bit of the Dover Straits. On May 29 in the early evening she sighted a curious object two miles southeast of the S. Goodwin Light Vessel, discovered it to be one of our deserted Fleet Air Arm 'planes, made fast a line to its tail and slowly began towing it to harbour. Anyone who has attempted such a task knows that the semi-sunken aircraft is a brute to be hauled but this one was worse than most, for half an hour later out from a rack beneath the wing dropped a bomb which fortunately exploded well astern, and most of two hours later the stem of this 'plane parted from its body and sank, though Captain W. Hoiles marked the position.

Next day, more trouble. It was foggy weather when, shortly after daybreak, one of the Dutch *schuyts* taken over by the Admiralty coming back from Dunkirk full of soldiers broke down and had to be towed into harbour. Out came the "Kenia" again and took in tow the Motor Yacht "Inspiration", which was drifting abandoned with the tide. A couple more motor launches were found the following day likewise deserted, and also had to be brought in. Then came the fourth, and most surprising, of these eventful occasions. It began with the unhappy distant picture of a Swedish vessel sinking, and just before dusk on June 2 a sailing barge could be descried some 2½ miles southeast of the South Goodwins L.V. The stranger needed assistance, but what brought her there?

On coming alongside her, the "Kenia" saw that she was none other than the "Ena", of which we have previously made mention,[7] and we last saw her lying off Dunkirk abandoned to fate. Somehow members of the B.E.F. there had got aboard, not one of them was a sailor; yet difficult as the rig is for even the professional, or highly experienced amateur yachtsman, this crew of warriors without any assistance managed to bring "Ena" and themselves all those miles from the French coast through bombs and shells to the position indicated. Don't ask me why, or how it was done. If the incident were not perfectly authenticated, it would seem beyond all credence. It is sufficient to state that the tug "Kenia" took her in tow for a few short miles, and anchored her a quarter of a mile from the harbour.

We mentioned just now the "Vincia", another of Messrs. William Watkins' tugs which so distinguished themselves on the Dunkirk occasion. She had been lying in the Downs when, the last afternoon of May, she was sent towing three ships' life-boats across to Dunkirk very much needed just then. An odd thing happened on passing the Sandettie Buoy when out of the sky to the open sea descended a parachutist, whereupon "Vincia" steamed to pick him up. He turned out to be a British gunner, who had 'baled out' after being in combat with a Nazi. Unfortunately the man was badly wounded, so seeing the destroyer H.M.S. "Venomous" not far distant, they took him over aboard her before continuing to Bray.

Anchoring off the latter about 9 p.m., the "Vincia" sent all the ship's life-boats and her own manned by the tug's crew, who did excellent work for the next six hours, and brought most of three hundred soldiers aboard. She was on her way down the roadstead bound for England when H.M.S. "Keith", destroyer just mentioned, ordered the troops to be transferred aboard another destroyer, whilst "Vincia" was to remain at Bray fetching off some others.

It was at 8-15 a.m. in full daylight, June 1, that the "Keith" (Captain E. L. Berthon, R.N.) was badly hit in a bombing raid. "Vincia" went to her help and rescued 108, who included naval officers and ratings, some of the British G.H.Q. staff and some also of the French G.H.Q., whilst not far away another destroyer was blown to pieces with the loss of all hands.

Search through the pages of naval history from the earliest to the present time, and it would not be possible to find any sort of occurrence comparable with this Dunkirk withdrawal, still less such unity of unprepared crews toiling so strenuously on behalf of professional soldiers. The Epic of Dunkirk! How amazing it all seems every time we reconsider the matter! How surpassing everything that we might ever have imagined!

These tugmasters are known the world over for their brilliance in taking liners in or out of dock, despite our powerful tides; they are summoned to salve a steamer which has fallen on bad times after collision or stranding. They are ready always with pumps and hoses to put out a fire burning down below.

But so totally different was this rescue service of ships and soldiers. Not for any except a big, national purpose was the Thames denuded of those able, extremely seaworthy, little ships sent out with the least warning on a mission very different from their role of nudging steamers round awkward corners out of the tideway into quiet basins. A mere glance along the river proved that something very unordinary was at work.

But the unending procession from our white cliffs to the sand dunes of France was something which the seagulls could not comprehend, and the Germans daily waxed more angry that try as they might this persistent help to our forces could not be blotted out.

When the tug "Java" went across in company with three drifters and four motorboats, it needed a good deal more than mere common sense. At dawn, whilst the latter tried getting into the beaches, they were thwarted by draught, so the tug had to send her own boat with only the Mate and a deckhand to pick up soldiers that were transferred first to motorboats, thence to drifters or tug. It wasted much valuable time, but when the well-filled tug placed her batch of troops into the 4200 tons cruiser H.M.S. "Calcutta" off La Panne, she kept filling up again from the beaches till there was no other vessel waiting and "Java" must bring the men over to England.

Five miles after leaving Dunkirk, the "Java" observed a 'plane in the sea, and the sailors having been so brutally bombed made sure here was another German whom they could scarcely be restrained from hitting with the guns. He was British, right enough, as also was the other man in her, so Captain W. Jones took them both on board, and after another mile found soldiers clinging to some wreckage or swimming about. They owed their lives to the keen crew who, for sixty consecutive hours without sleep or stop, had laboured of their best. Their clothes they gave to tattered soldiers, their own stores to any who were still hungry and, having saved lives from the wrecked paddle steamer "Waverley" were able to land at Ramsgate 250 weary and tired troops.

There was even more that tugs longed to perform, as, for instance, when H.M. Trawler "Jacinta" became stranded on the wreck of another vessel and threatened to capsize, but they could not be everywhere at the same time. To give some idea of what was being required, let it be understood that all this while there existed so much shipping in Dover harbour, the demands on tugs for controlling and assisting seemed enormous.

During the busiest period of the Dunkirk evacuation there were as many as eighteen ships of various kinds using the Admiralty Pier simultaneously at Dover. Almost as fast as vessels could land their hundreds or thousands, they turned round and went to France again, having stopped only to water or bunker. It was highly important that there should be no delay in landing the troops, so practically every craft needed to have a tug's assistance whilst the inside steamer was getting away or shifted berth to make room for others. By no means unusual, therefore, was the employment of two tugs per berthing ship.

Those who know the hot tides both at the eastern and western end of Dover, the never ceasing surge and swell inside on the finest days, will not be surprised at the immense amount of work which now became there requisite for the four tugs "Simla", "Gondia", "Roman" and "Lady Brassey". But, apart from this special rush of Dunkirk days, there was a more or less steady duty for these tugs when shifting units to be repaired at Dover in what is known as the Submarine Camber Dock, the Granville, or Wellington Dock.

There were forty or more buoys in the main harbour, tugs being required for berthing at these, for conveying stores and ammunition to men-of-war: in fact during the last fortnight of May the "Simla" assisted in or out of Dover at least 140 ships. It was good to find these crews, though hardly getting a wink of sleep, never grumbling but carrying on with the work of ensuring speedy disembarkation of the returning troops.

But always the unsuspected incident would crop up. The French S.S. "Themsen" full of refugees had collided with the British S.S. "Efford" three miles southwest of Dover, where tide and traffic at the best of times are bad enough. Well, the "Efford" on May 22 sank and her crew were rowing about in one of her life-boats till the "Simla" came out and rescued them.

It appeared that the "Themsen" had run right into the "Efford" and that the former's Captain, after being bombed all day off Dunkirk, was in such a nervous condition that he could not take further charge of her, so he asked the Captain of "Simla" to go aboard and pilot "Themsen" in whilst "Simla" (in charge of the Mate) towed in the Frenchman.

Many exhausted crews had every reason at Dover for thanking tugmen. In the early hours of May 24 the two destroyers H.M.S. "Whitshed" and "Vimy" were lying at Admiralty Pier when orders came for shifting berth to buoys. From their recent Dunkirk experiences these naval men were utterly played out, so the tugs let them doze on and moved the destroyers unaided. You can imagine, after their deep and much needed sleep, they were surprised to note the new location.

We had reason to mention in another chapter the S.S. "Kohistan", 5884 tons, which with about six thousand troops aboard was waiting to be berthed at the Admiralty Pier. It had to be done quickly because of the enemy aeroplanes around, but it was so dark a night, the harbour so full of other ships, no one being allowed to show any navigating illuminant, that the task could not be envied. When the "Simla" and "Lady Brassey" were trying, it was just like working in a thick fog. You could not see ships or buoys, there would first be a scraping along one destroyer, then missing the next by a few feet, but it was all cleverly effected and the soldiers got ashore safely.

What did these tugs do in and out of Dover harbour? They did everything.

On May 27 one of the former Isle of Man steam packets got to within five or six miles of Dover in bad condition. The Dunkirk 'planes had bombed her and killed forty soldiers and wounded seventy on the upper deck, and the damaged ship had been saved only by our destroyers driving away the enemy. The "Simla" and "Lady Brassey" were able to bring this broken-down transport into harbour, and a similar job was done next day by the same pair of tugs when they went to succour H.M.S. "Montrose", a 1530 tons flotilla leader full of troops, but with her bow damaged.

These days at the end of May and early the next month were one long-drawn-out uncertainty. Nothing was improbable, everything was possible. It might be H.M.S. "Jaguar", so recently a smart, new destroyer but now after being bombed badly making water and wanting assistance from the tugs to be brought into Dover. Or it might be H.M.S. "Bideford", a 1105 tons British sloop full of French soldiers arriving with her stern blown off, twenty-five men killed and others wounded. The "Simla" must tow her in through the pier-heads and place her inside the Submarine Dock. Or, again it might be yet another destroyer, H.M.S. "Impulsive", with starboard engine out of control.

It was just bad luck on June 1 that the cross-Channel steamer "Maid of Orleans" on leaving Admiralty Pier should when rounding the Prince of Wales Pier collide with such force that a 1120 tons destroyer almost capsized, throwing twenty soldiers into the water, some being drowned. A sad sequel to having been through a bad campaign and just arrived from Dunkirk.

CHAPTER XVII — BY MIGHT AND MAIN

THOSE tugs watching and patrolling near the Downs saw plenty of incidents to prevent monotony. The tug "Doria" on May 30 noticed the S.S. "Shaftesbury" on the SW Goodwins, and after some hours managed to get her afloat. Next day she was putting out a fire which had broken out in a petrol craft, or piloting into harbour both French steam and motor trawlers.

But June 3 from midnight was too unhappy an occasion for pleasant lingering memories. It was the arrival of the previously mentioned "Royal Daffodil", whose dead and wounded had to be brought ashore, whilst sand, cement and timber had to be fetched off to her for essential repairs. Unable any longer to use her engines, the "Royal Daffodil" was towed by "Doria" to Dover with the salvage steamer "Forde" alongside helping.

Our great debt of gratitude is that these tugs supply us with so many details which otherwise would be missed, when commanding officers of a bigger ship had more than enough to occupy all their thoughts. Here and there are little touches that help to complete the great canvas depicting all which Dunkirk meant.

The "Lady Brassey" steaming from Dover to get the damaged flotilla leader H.M.S. V Montrose" from the range of German searchlights that dominated Gris Nez, and towing her stern first; next day missing H.M.S. "Bideford" in the fog, but also missing the bombs which deluged down off Gravelines; towing the injured "Prague" till she grounded comfortably; assisting trawlers which had got ashore and then taking in tow a destroyer that lay battered, helpless, but full of troops: these are real-life episodes which might be forgotten unless set down whilst we have the knowledge.

We know by this means what a job the "Prague" on the night of May 30 was having to get clear of East Dunkirk jetty when "Foremost 87" and "Lady Brassey" just succeeded in towing the bigger vessel afloat, and there could not have been more than one foot of water under the

"Prague's" bottom, but a trawler wreck astern was showing an anchor light burning as guide to be avoided.

It is a desperate contemplation as we look back on that very dark night with bombs, bullets, and bits of shrapnel buzzing over the bridge. Here was "Foremost" tugging from the "Prague's" bows, the "Lady Brassey" at the stern, but unfortunately the latter's wire was not adequately made fast and it slipped off till re-secured. How through this murk and intense traffic the two tugs brought the "Prague" clear of the trawler-wreck, out through the two jetties, and swung her into the fairway is a question which can be answered by these crews alone. Then, having cast her off, there was still work to be done guiding other ships inside.

Some of these tugs had experience both at Calais and Boulogne. Outside the last-mentioned harbour the tug "Gondia" narrowly escaped sinking by bombs when a Heinkel was shot down within a hundred yards as it essayed destroying the S.S. "Groningen". The "Gondia" got away from Boulogne on the night of May 21 with over a hundred officers and men, though snipers and traitors were active from the shore.

After the tug "Empire Henchman" was sent from Dover to Dunkirk on the last day of May, she towed a barge laden with provisions and ammunition for the gallant defenders, but on the next day was prevented by a formation of twenty aeroplanes off Dunkirk. It is worthy of note that though neither tug nor barge was actually hit, the bombs fell in such shallow water, and created such violent concussions, that fractures occurred in "Empire Henchman's" fuel tanks, which in turn caused leaking fuel into the bilges to bring about serious risk of fire. Moreover the shock did grave damage as well to her electric installation and pumps as to her compasses.

It was therefore deemed advisable to return towards Dover, where the barge was seen to be leaking badly, and the partial disablement of "Empire Henchman" necessitated the tug being sent to another corner of the coast. Such is the ability of modern explosives, that at present the race is rather to them than to steam tugs, destroyers, paddlers — or what you will. Yet it would hardly be fair to claim that warfare no longer is the game for high stakes, that seamanship and the handling of craft has become merely mechanical.

We know that is not the case, that Dunkirk proved there never was such a need for personal bravery, and obtaining the best results by knowing just how much your own ship is capable of doing. The work of these tugmasters is stressed for the reason that they most especially have handed down through the development of steam those qualities which we most respected under sail. They are accustomed to difficult jobs, frequently they had to go abroad and fetch a disabled vessel home, salvage duties never worried them, much of the former colourful romance has given way to hard scientific business. Yet fundamentally these tugs depend on the human element of skill and endurance, of intimate knowledge with one of the most highly specialised sections of seafaring.

But the area of the Thames, the Downs, with an occasional trip into Dunkirk Roads were before this war very much the sphere of the tugmaster, so that these craft were employed in their very element when this great evacuation called them. Admittedly, that space between the Dunkirk breakwaters was an impossible bit of water to ask any decent ship to back and fill, to take off the many thousand soldiers: yet these little tugs were so accustomed at all states of the Thames tide to operate in worse places.

All their lives these men and craft have been wont to do the cleverest things with big ships and their buoys, running ropes out to wharves, berthing vessels that must lie with head upstream, nursing the greatest tonnage round awkward narrow bends of the river. Such units as "Kenia" or "Gondia" were too accustomed to all sorts of work, carrying stores and passengers, that really Dunkirk — apart from the aerial activity — was not much out of the ordinary.

So in one form or another there was every need for tugs, both because the southeastern region is part of the British war area generally, and because Hitler in his advance made a great bid for the Channel ports that confronted our island. Where tugs were needed for looking after the Downs in those first nine months of hostilities, they were doubly demanded to be sent round from the Thames to help our shipping during the Dunkirk crisis. It has been said that during those hectic days the river was denuded of tugs, but at any rate it is true from the list to be gathered from preceding pages that the number was considerable. Let there be added to the general usage such experts in towing as the "Crested Cock", the "Ocean Cock", the famous "Sun III", "Sun IV", "Sun VII", "Sun, VIII", "Sun X", "Sun XI", "Sun XII", "Sun XV", the "Fairplay I", and the "Contest". They represent a fleet of immense financial and strategic value.

But the greatest thing about them is that they were immediately ready.

Thus when Captain H. R. Cole was sent on June 1 in one of the "Sun" class, towing twenty ship's life-boats from the Thames to Ramsgate, and, asked whether he and his crew would care to go across to try and rescue soldiers from Dunkirk beaches, there came immediate volunteering. Towing, this time, two of the boats with also a motor craft, the vessel made a night passage. The latter at first anchored off the port when Captain Cole was asked by a British naval officer the following question after the three boats had brought some forty British soldiers from the beach.

"Do you happen to be acquainted with Dunkirk?"

"A little. I was serving there with the Inland Water Transport in the last war."

That was excellent. So anchor was hove up, the tug nosed alongside the pierhead, and she took off therefrom 50 more French and Belgians, including a Belgian Lieut.- Colonel. Presently she came out, the launch added more to the number, and altogether she left for England with over two hundred.

The "Sun III" after towing on May 31 the four sailing barges "Haste-Away", "Ada Mary", "Shannon", and "Burton" to Ramsgate and thence in the direction of Dunkirk, had only a very old chart not marked with the danger areas. As related on a previous page, she followed at first astern of the "Fishbourne" train ferry, but there was the nuisance of barges breaking adrift and being picked up, and we related that the tugs "Duke", "Prince" and "Princess" were also helping. We must not forget that the "Sun III" when approaching the French coast picked up boats containing our fighters by co-operation with British aeroplanes. In all this tug saved 148 officers and men, and got them back to Ramsgate.

Frankly the towing of these barges was somewhat of a nuisance, their frequent breaking away from snapped tow-ropes enough to try the patience of any Skipper, so, having brought them back, the "Sun III" proceeded to her normal work. It cannot be said that this barge idea was a great success, and Captains of tugs were never happy about that endeavour. The rope made fast to the "Shannon" even pulled the windlass right out of the deck, and overboard disappeared the whole

150

winding arrangement. Much better was the scheme of allowing a free hand for these tugs to operate individually and pick up all the men possible.

The "Sun IV" brought a dozen life-boats and crews (not, of course, the R.N.L.I.) from Tilbury to Ramsgate which were sent to Dunkirk in batches, this vessel taking nine thereto. It is extraordinary how repeatedly masters of craft emphasise the wash of high-powered vessels both en route and in the Dunkirk vicinity. A destroyer in the latter was the cause of hurling a couple of sailors into the sea, and though "Sun IV" quickly let go her boats astern and made for the spot, only one man was saved. During her return voyage with three life-boats in tow, one was swamped by the wash of destroyers fighting an air attack, and 2½ hours later yet another was similarly sunk by a different destroyer.

What the bargemen humorously described as "Brock's benefit" happened during the hours of June 1-2 in Dunkirk harbour. The coming back was far from a pleasant yachting trip. Despite the banging and crashing of bombs and guns, this "Sun" had rescued 112 B.E.F. who were on board, another 39 she was towing in the R.N.L.I. boat "Edme" (which also she had piloted into harbour), and another life-boat with more troops was likewise being towed astern full of people.

It was a weird, eerie experience coming out of that pitch-black Dunkirk with shells to right and left, the fumes and thick pall of smoke. Cluttered up by so many passengers and a couple of heavy tows, no wonder that the "Sun IV" was difficult to handle, that she picked up the mud. Several times she bumped also on the bottom, but brought her party to Ramsgate, though the "Edme's" coxswain had been killed. Off went "Sun IV" again to look for the hospital ship "Paris", only to discover her abandoned.

Again "Sun IV" was off, towing this time four motor launches, sighted two magnetic mines off the North Goodwin L.V. and got a sloop to sink them, loaded up some more passengers on the night of June 3-4 at Dunkirk, assisted H.M.S. "Malcolm" — the last destroyer to take troops out of that harbour — then dodged the violent bombing and streaked across to Ramsgate again. By this time Dunkirk was evacuated fully, and she could go on with her usual River jobs.

No wonder that naval officers on the spot spoke of these various tugs with admiration, no wonder that soldiers could hardly find words sufficiently full of gratitude. It was the "Sun VII" which towed five

R.A.F. boats from Dover to Dunkirk and six times had to stop and pick them up broken adrift. The "Sun VIII" brought a dozen ship's boats on May 30 from Tilbury by night to Ramsgate.

Next day, with a convoy of tugs and trawlers, she made a passage to Dunkirk and timed her arrival there after dark on May 31, being assigned the beach at Bray dunes. Dunkirk itself resembled a shambles with fires raging and smoke fuming over a thousand feet high, yet the NE wind kept the beach clear. A short tiresome swell was running when "Sun VIII" anchored, tide ebbing, and the boats were sent in to the sands. These did their duties so well that they rowed refugees aboard the sloops, and when the sloops were filled it was possible to crowd the decks of "Sun VIII" so that she could get away before daybreak. And about time, too, for she had begun bumping the ground on that swell. Speed! That had been the night's motto, that was the inspiration to the end; for the other tugs had departed, some of the boats being handed over to a sloop, and the rest were abandoned before 4-30 a.m. so as not to delay the tug's passage down the roadstead. By this time the wind had shifted, coming off the land, which made it more difficult than ever for, besides the bombing attacks, the smoke blew. West of the pierheads the big fires emitted their dark clouds over a sea littered with wrecks and abandoned shipping. It was not without a sense of relief that "Sun VIII" arrived at Ramsgate with one hundred and twenty troops alive.

But we have nearly finished our story of these tugs, which so satisfactorily performed the dual purpose of bringing boats to the beaches and of doing the odd jobs shifting steamers to berths inside Dunkirk jetties. The "Sun X" with three other tugs brought four boats from Dover, and the usual breaking adrift on passage was inevitable. In vain the "Sun X" tried to assist a transport that had grounded fully loaded with soldiers inside Dunkirk piers, for a cast of the lead disclosed only 10 feet and the transport was still 200 feet away.

But the tug went on with her boat-loading, collected 300 troops, and again went into the harbour and pushed transports along the jetties as if it had been the Tilbury Landing Stage or some Thames lockgate. Then with the oncoming of that third of June the "Sun X" could go home. Her sister, the "Sun XI", after bringing three sailing barges from Tilbury to Dover, set out for Dunkirk towing a lighter (full of stores and petrol cans containing drinking water) and one barge. The latter was finally beached, but the fun began when "Jerry" started dropping his gifts and blew up one of H.M. Drifters, whose crew the tug "Contest" picked up.

The "Sun XI" got thence to Dover, but at midnight of June 1-2 there was a rare sight for anyone capable of being impressed. Seven tugs in single line ahead! "Ocean Cock", "Crested Cock", "Challenge", "Fairplay I", "Sun VII", "Sun XI", and "Sun XII" all steaming bound for the scene of horror if intent on their duties. Yet the "Sun XI" had to drop out before the end. For about 2 a.m. she sighted the unusual glow of small lights, and then someone with a dimmed morse was flashing signals.

Captain J. R. Lukes therefore swung his wheel hard astarboard, and headed "Sun XI" towards the stranger. Coming alongside, he saw it was a large Government lighter which had completely broken down. Full of wounded and troops, they were survivors of a British destroyer which had been blown up, and a few hours later the "Sun XI" brought that lighter with its sad occupants to Dover.

During these final Evacuation days the Channel was full of surprises; any day or night might reveal boats in distress with motors no longer working and men barely clinging to life. On June 2 Captain Lukes was off again towing four motorboats towards Dunkirk, followed by three more tugs. Of these the "Foremost 87" soon spotted half a dozen life-boats full of wounded and survivors of sunken ships, so turned back with them. In Dunkirk the usual medley of ships arriving presented itself, transports wanting to depart, tugs aground at low water, others jammed tightly full of troops, still more towing completely filled life-boats.

Finally the first streaks of dawn, the rising of the tide, full speed ahead for the Kentish shores, a bump and thud, and never did the North Goodwin lightship in the early light look so good and welcome.

The "Sun XII" (Captain B. R. Mastin) came from Tilbury to Dover with four barges, and with "Fairplay I" on June 1 left towing the "Ethel Everard" and "Tollesbury", which the reader will recollect being beached off Bray Dunes. Captain Mastin says "the firework display was undescribable" there, but about 4 a.m. a naval officer told them "to get to hell out of it as quick as we could". It had become quite impossible at this corner, the soldiers could no longer be safely taken aboard till further west, so they returned to Dover and the seven ("Fairplay I", "Ocean Cock", "Foremost 89", "Contest", "Sun VII", "Sun XI" and "Sun XII") again made the attempt that night, though once more they were ordered back to Dover. There was other work for them to do.

If these tugs, then, had contributed nothing else than towing the collected miscellany of boats from Tilbury first to a Kentish port then over to the French coast, they would admirably have fulfilled their purpose, and those which fetched the barges or the train-ferry were performing most difficult tasks. But it is especially in respect of their collecting so many soldiers, or enabling the transports to get in and out of the jetties, that we must always think of these little steamers gladly.

The "Sun XV", after being demagnetized, towed a dozen boats round to Ramsgate, so it was quite a valuable accumulation which these tugs brought from the Thames, and of these the "Sun XV" brought six thence to Dunkirk, or more accurately, La Panne. It was a hard night that first of June, not merely because of the bombers but the German artillery of all calibres and the surf. Nevertheless, about eighty soldiers were gathered aboard, even if all the boats save one was lost, and so they got home.

On the following evening when sent out to rescue the hospital ship "Paris", the latter was found badly listing to starboard, the last survivor had gone, but the tug had only got her wire fast when heavy machine-gun fire spattered from the sky and the wire broke. It was forbidden to continue, though this tug next sighted the H.M. Drifter "Yorkshire Lass" further west, loaded with troops yet hampered with temporary engine trouble. Back once more steamed "Sun XV", and was actually alongside that eastern Dunkirk pier in the early hours of June 4. Practically all had embarked, the Great Evacuation completed, and it remained only to get away at full speed through bullets, bombs, and shells before dawn should reveal her. On the way, luckily, this "Sun XV" was able to pass close to another of H.M. Drifters — this time, the "L.H.W.D." which had developed engine trouble — and she was towed to Ramsgate.

Some tugs were more lucky than others, though all were indispensable. The "Racia" brought a dozen tugs to the beaches, sent them ashore and loaded up with soldiers for Ramsgate. On that final morning of June 4 she was placing her ladders alongside the jetty for French soldiers to climb down, and after that she helped the last of our destroyers before quitting the place at 2-45 a.m. Out in the Dyck Channel the "Racia" stopped only to take the crew and a wounded soldier out of a motor launch.

Then one more of our destroyers passed, and someone from the bridge sang out:

"Put on all the speed you can, and hurry back home."

The "Racia" needed no second admonishing. She got her soldiers safely into Ramsgate.

Now we have seen one notable hazard inside the Dunkirk jetties was lack of depth, apart from lack of breadth. The "Foremost 22" drew, for example, 13 feet aft, which was quite a consideration after half ebb. The previously mentioned collision just past 11 p.m. between "St. Helier" and H.M.S. "Sharpshooter", the 835 tons minesweeper, was an opportunity that gave "Foremost 22" the chance of passing a tow-rope to "Sharpshooter This consisted of 60 fathoms 16-inch manilla shackled to 50 fathoms of 5-inch wire, the end of the latter being made fast to the "Sharpshooter's" stern whilst the manilla end was on the tug's towing hook.

All this had to be done with care because of the warship's depth charges at the stern, and she had been hit just forward of her bridge, yet despite the crumpled bows the tug was able to bring that destroyer all the way to Dover: about 50 miles in 13 hours. But for this assistance, it is humanly certain that the partially disabled "Sharpshooter" would have fallen an easy target alike to the enemy aircraft and the shore batteries.

When on Sunday night, June 2, the "Foremost 22" once more entered Dunkirk harbour and there found the S.S. "Newhaven" aground, it was quite a tough proposition what to do. Tide was ebbing and the tug got her tow-rope to "Newhaven", but went ashore herself. By a great effort the former's engines allowed her to float off, proceed out of the harbour and send to "Newhaven" a tug of less draught. Motorboats having brought French troops to the tug, she set out with them to Dover, by which time the crew were utterly played out. In short, these tugs were able to render so many and different services both to ships of the Royal Navy and to their brothers of the Merchant Navy, that it is unthinkable the Dunkirk withdrawal without such help might have been far less possible. The handling of a tug, like that of a Thames barge, is not acquired at once but demands a lifetime under all weathers in all conditions.

That all this seamanlike skill should have been placed at the nation's use is both a reason for our congratulation and a source of great thankfulness.

CHAPTER XVIII — ENTERPRISE AND COURAGE

DURING these Dunkirk activities all sorts of treachery were being attempted in the town, along the beaches, and even afloat.

Fifth columnists would indicate targets to the German 5.9-inch guns though seven miles distant. It was done by firing rockets from the harbour's tall lighthouse, which being 187 feet commanded the surrounding flat country quite easily. All that the enemy needed was to aim slightly east of this circular erection and shells could not miss falling on the pier's concrete. Aim a little to the west, and they would deluge the invisible beaches.

Of course the Germans made some ludicrous mistakes. The hulls of three vessels lying off the harbour considerably intrigued certain Nazis who imagined that troops were about to be transported. Actually these were wrecks in shallow water!

So, too, less than four miles northeast of the entrance lay a steamer, which Nazi bombers attacked over and over again. Yet she would not sink. For here extends that shoal patch marked on the chart as Hills Bank, which in places dries right out at low water but covered at high tide. In past years I have known several craft thus to be picked up, but somehow the enemy could not understand that a transport having got her bilge on the hard sand would never sink.

One of the most impressive features was the flaring of the oil-tanks in the harbour when two million gallons of petrol blazed their flames skywards and were seen by people living in Kent. The pall of smoke for days hampered the Germans, though it did not interrupt the designs of traitors. Two further instances will suffice.

Waiting on Dunkirk beach for a boat was a party of twenty-five French soldiers whom a civilian approached and began making pleasant conversation. Having ingratiated himself and aroused no suspicion, suddenly he whipped out a "Tommy" gun and began filling the Frenchmen with lead. All except four. These were quick enough on the uptake to use the same tactics and shoot life out of him.

You never knew friend from foe in those dizzy days. One small British steamer had taken on board a full complement of passengers, principally French wounded troops, but among these were a dozen strangers who mingled with the crowd and seemed ordinary enough. Actually they were Germans disguised in French uniforms.

Barely had the ship cleared the roadstead and gained the open sea than this bunch of gangsters produced twelve automatic pistols, aimed at the bridge and shot the captain, who fell to the deck mortally wounded.

Simultaneously they shot the signaller, who showed himself a brave and resourceful sailor. Dragging himself painfully to the speaking-tube, he whispered below to where seven of the crew happened to be.

"Armed Germans have taken the ship ..." he managed to utter. "... Come on up with revolvers."

And, having thus expended his dying breath, he too collapsed. Yet all was not over.

The sound of heavy treads indicated that seven men were racing to their shipmates' assistance. Their fury and indignation at such treachery composed one dominating passion and they killed the Nazis forthwith. Meanwhile the ship carried on towards England.

Until the troops had gone ashore, the suffering captain held on to life with a great and bitter struggle. Then, faithful to the very end, he sat down and wrote a special report commending his men for their bravery; which, being done, he shortly afterwards died.

The entrance into Dunkirk's harbour is between two jetties. They had been built, as we saw, not for embarkation purposes, but simply as breakwaters with open pilework through which the three-knot tide gurgled and rose even sixteen to nineteen feet. Worn-out warriors, heavy with gun and accoutrement, slid rather than climbed down to heaving decks. Mess-tables were fetched up for gangways, scaling ladders had to be employed. Between shell-bursts against the concrete a few stretcher cases could be conveniently lifted at low water aboard a destroyer, since her forebridge would be then level with the top.

The sight of these long, lean war vessels speeding into this restricted space was a lesson in ship-handling. Under way, or alongside this pier, their guns rarely stopped barking, or hulls ceased to shake from the recoil as each yellow burst of cordite interrupted the naval surgeon busy with his tourniquet, whilst bluejackets were slicing loaves of bread and bully beef for ravenous troops.

But there was a certain mercantile steamer, whose master chanced to be as gallant as nature had made him independent. A real, hard-case, unquenchable sailor-man, who knew his mind — and spoke it.

A soldier clambering aboard began — with the best of intentions — helping the crew to haul in a hawser.

Suddenly the roar of thunder, and the sound of an earthquake, came from the direction of the bridge.

"Hey, you!"

The soldier realised he was being addressed. An oldish man in a peaked cap bellowed.

"You drop that hawser", insisted the irate skipper. "My men can run their own ship. You come and work this damn gun. That's your job."

And the soldier, with several of his pals, now worked it against Nazi bombers to some purpose.

Later on, after the steamer was in mid-channel, a khaki passenger dared to inquire who might be the captain.

"That bloke what ticked you off just now? Oh! he's all right, but he doesn't like a landsman interfering. Sixty-seven years. And still tough."

"I'll believe it."

"Doesn't know the word fear ... but you remember him? Kept on running Franco's blockade a little while back in the Spanish war. Now he's running daily trips to Dunkirk. And enjoying every minute."

"What's his name?"

"Jones. Captain 'Potato' Jones. German 'plane broke his shoulder three months ago, but he can't keep off the sea."

Conditions became awkward when the enemy by mounting heavy batteries ashore made the direct route past Calais impracticable. A fresh course had to be ruled on the charts, and when that way likewise became compromised, still a third approach was cleared across the shoals by minesweepers and buoyed as a safe passage. After the daylight raids restricted evacuation to night, and to vessels of not less than 15-knots, it was still possible to send 30,000 troops away between dusk and dawn.

Those were days when human lives were being cast towards the English shore like bits of jetsam. Never in modern times had it been so necessary to keep an eye lifting for odd sorts of shipping, which might loom up any hour. Especially near the Downs, with the shifting shoals and strong tides. On the night of June 2 a disabled motorboat with fifteen exhausted British soldiers drifted perilously thither until the life-boat spotted them in time. Three mornings later this same rescuer brought in a boat containing two British, two Belgian, and thirteen Frenchmen in the last condition of fatigue. They had rowed all the way from Dunkirk.

In the most strange fashion comedy was mingled with the tragic. We lost six of our destroyers during the evacuation, and the captain of one found himself swimming about in a thick film of oil. Then, luckily, he was picked up by another vessel where his ruined uniform could be exchanged for a blanket and a pair of flannel trousers.

But what he most desired was to cleanse his body of this sticky fuel.

Barely had he got out of a hot bath than a heavy bomb 'whirooped' on to this second ship, went through bath and hull alike, leaving him once more swimming the sea.

Unlucky? Not a bit. Less than half a mile away he sighted yet another vessel, struck out towards her and was hoisted aboard once again.

Except for those who come from the families of Breton fishermen, French soldiers have a horror of the sea. In order to avoid being drowned some *poilus* contrived a strange invention. Ripping out the inner tubes from the tyres of Dunkirk's derelict lorries, they inflated the rubbers to form lifebelts and placed them round the waist. So they floated out to the boats.

Great idea! But when once aboard the crowded transport, where every millimetre of space had to be economised, this superfluous corpulence could not be tolerated. The living and the half-dead, the cheery and half-asleep, packed tight like pieces in a jig-saw puzzle, had still to make room for more. So, with apologies and a sharp knife, a seafaring officer walked round slitting every rubber tube flat.

Coincidences? Admittedly we had more than a little luck, yet what about that Nazi aviator who did something which might not happen once in ten million attempts? He himself would be the first to admit the chance. He aimed at a British transport, the bomb descended — but neither on the deck nor the bridge. It went, as we saw, down the funnel, without touching the sides, and never exploded till it got below.

Throughout those fateful days and nights, when death was cheap and glory hard won, the seamen of Britain and France pulled together as if at one rope. Lying in Dunkirk, waiting to leave the congested harbour-entrance, was a French steamer and nearby one of our minesweepers.

Whoop from the sky roared Nazi warplanes, which so effectually deluged the French decks that dozens of men were wounded, others blown into the water, and the ship looked more ghastly than can be conveyed by such words as slaughter and massacre.

Without hesitation, the British minesweeper sent off her whalers and these boats rowed among the floating debris of suffering men. Out of the water they performed some gallant rescuing, picked up the French captain and brought him aboard their own ship. Yes, he was alive, but the poor fellow's legs had been blown off at the knees.

Tenderly they laid him on deck, tried to make him as comfortable as the harsh circumstances allowed, and covered his bleeding body.

But his spirit burned within him ardently. Physical agony could not overpower his will. Gratitude from one seafarer to another must be his last expression before quitting existence.

With a valiant effort, he struggled to rise. His lips moved.

"Vive la Marine Anglaise!" he spoke. "Vive la …!"

Then he fell back. And death released him.

Apart from that large and assorted fleet of British and French warships, passenger-steamers, freighters, trawlers, drifters, tugs, paddlers, yachts and motorboats, were numbers of Belgian and Dutch craft which had rushed to England when first the Low Countries became invaded. That international assembly was symbolic of the hatred against German tyranny.

But the patient pluck of our own sailormen? There was one master mariner who, whilst crossing the Channel, had to endure the attacks of dive-bombers six times before reaching Dunkirk roadstead. There he remained at anchor, waiting his turn, while other ships were embarking their quota. All the while his guns with anti-aircraft fire were protecting the vessels inside.

Then at last came his turn to load up, and come out full of troops.

It was the opportunity for twelve determined Nazi planes to hurl their missiles. How his ship escaped receiving a direct hit, or any man being wounded, is hard to believe. One fairly near explosion, however, did burst the steampipe so that the ship lost way and fell out of control. The tide would have carried her on to the off-lying shoals had not a second steamer gallantly taken her in tow.

This the German perceived, so made a fresh swoop to destroy both.

"I'm not going to let two ships be sunk, when one is enough", reasoned the first captain. He transferred his soldiers to the rescuer, anchored clear of the shoal, swung to the tide and let his fellow mariner carry on towards England.

Engineers set to work on the steampipe, one attack after another poured from the sky at the stationary target. And this continued for ninety exciting minutes.

So far not one bomb made a hit, but such rare fortune would surely run out.

Men toiled hopefully, but under most discouraging difficulties. Fate was giving them a raw deal. How could repairs be done whilst death might suddenly wipe out everybody.

Still, there might be a chance of giving "Jerry" a farewell adieu.

At last!

A good temporary job was finished, steam began to be raised, pressure rose, already the cable links rattled up through the hawse-hole. Then the engine-room telegraphs clanged, propellers started revolving, the ship going ahead.

Setting a course for the white cliffs of England, the steamer worked up to 20 knots. Devotion to duty, self-sacrifice and confidence had snatched another intended victim from the enemy's onslaught.

CHAPTER XIX — THE MIRACLE OF OUR AGE

WHAT shall we say of those wonderful women in Red Cross uniform who for days and nights endured the horrors of Dunkirk's beach, quietly tending wounded soldiers despite the bombs and shells and bullets?

All the while without sleep, toiling selflessly and refusing to accept evacuation until the last injured warrior had been sent afloat, the white-aproned figures were conspicuous targets for the murderous planes. Even whilst trying to drag dying men to a bit of shelter beneath the sandy hillocks, or moistening parched throats with tepid water, or helping walking cases to wade out into the boats, those noble heroines were given no respite by a cruel foe.

Thus to their martyrdom passed many a gallant soul. Deliberately of set purpose the Nazis attacked hospital ships, as for instance on that fine, clear, night of Sunday, June 2. An ex-passenger vessel, but plainly marked on her sides with the conspicuous Red Cross, came steaming for Dunkirk to fetch the sick, but whilst in mid-channel and two hours before sunset three bombers dived on her savagely at seven o'clock.

Besides captain and crew there were doctors and six voluntary nurses aboard. At eight o'clock the enemy again appeared, so the captain was putting the nurses into the ship's life-boat which was still swinging in the davits when one raider swooped low and sprayed his bullets at the helpless women.

More than one tired soldier on the spattered beach kept asking "What's happened to our R.A.F.?"

The answer is that with numerical inferiority they could not be everywhere, but by moral superiority our fighters broke up German air squadrons every time. And this sometimes brought about the most thrilling developments.

One British pilot over Dunkirk contended fiercely till the last of his ammunition ran out, when a couple of Messerschmitts loomed up on his tail. The only tactics now were to keep dodging the Germans' fusillade so far as possible, and this went on till one of them likewise had expended his ammunition and sheered off.

Unfortunately two more hostile 'planes arrived and kept firing short bursts unpleasantly close. For some while this went on, but eventually when forced down to 500 feet the British 'plane received a bullet in the engines and things looked ugly. Crashing on to the sea, some three miles from the coast, it capsized; but the aviator refused to give up hope. Inflating his "Mae West" (i.e. his lifesaving jacket), he climbed like a half-drowned terrier on to the machine's top, and drew a deep breath. It was good still to be alive.

But again the enemy spotted him and made another onslaught. This was avoided by slipping back into the water at the right moment beneath the tail of the sinking machine: so that finally the Nazi was fooled and made off, thinking his opponent to be dead.

Still, the Briton's position was not enviable. He hung on precariously, the minutes sped by, it needed only the sea to get boisterous and end the incident. Yet the incredible did happen as if it were a bit of fiction. For at the end of an hour this tiny speck on the water was sighted by one of H.M. sloops, the aviator was picked up, and twelve hours afterwards arrived back in his aerodrome none the worse for his exciting adventure.

Not less memorable was the experience of another pilot who had a busy battle against three enemy sky-scouts. Then four more soared overhead and did not improve his prospects. Perhaps he might yet fight his way through, so he fired a sharp burst which had the effect of sending the leading 'plane fluttering to earth, though the others redoubled their efforts and a running stream of bullets was being exchanged at high speed.

Such an unequal contest could not go on indefinitely. All too realistically smoke issuing from the lonely British machine conveyed its own implication: it was time to descend — on the land if possible, on the sea if nowhere else practicable. With professional skill and good fortune, he alighted his burning craft on the sands and a hasty inspection revealed a bullet in his machinery, control column smashed, and oil gushing out of the feed pipe.

Only one thing now remained, and he did it quickly. Setting his 'plane on fire, he wandered inland and came across one of the B.E.F. motor vehicles by which a lift was obtained into Dunkirk. His arrival there synchronised with an aerial bombardment, yet he survived that. And then? He looked about, found one of the paddle-steamers engaged withdrawing troops, and aboard her set off for home.

Even now there could be no peace. The ship cleared away from the smoking scene, down dived another Heinkel to bestow death, but the naval guns of a nearby destroyer took careful aim, hit the bomber fair and square and the German went hurtling through space into the sea. So at length from the city of ruined docks and warehouses, of streets gutted by fires, of roads hollowed out into craters, the pilot got home to England's fair and pleasant land.

And the R.A.F., apart from its fighting duties, was able to assist troops directly. On June 1 three American-built Hudson bombers were patrolling off Dunkirk when they sighted some forty German aircraft about to attack transports that were carrying homeward some hundreds of the B.E.F.

Without hesitation the Hudsons steered for the enemy and made a perfect clean-up. Inside thirteen brilliant minutes three Junkers dive-bombers were shot down, two others descended out of control, and the rest — having perceived that one of their number immolated himself in the blazing oil-tanks of the port and that another reached the sea in fragments — decided it were healthier to give up the contest.

Those transports had been spared almost certain destruction.

A little later the leader of this British flight saw not far from the roadstead a couple of life-boats full of troops, but drifting helplessly with the tide. One Hudson therefore was assigned to keep watch, whilst the others flew in various directions seeking aid on the sea. At length they observed two tugs, signalled them and sent them to the boats, which were recovered. Scarcely had this been directed than out of a cloud raced eight Nazi bombers intent on destroying these boats.

But those Germans simply hadn't the magnificent ardour which inspired our fellows, for when one Hudson made for them alone, all eight promptly disappeared across the sky.

One of the smaller vessels that had been hurriedly sent from England had the misfortune to be abandoned through an accident whilst only three-quarters of the way across. Along came a Dutch vessel which enabled the disappointed crew none the less to reach Dunkirk, where they spent seventeen ceaseless hours rowing troops from beach to shipping, but simultaneously suffering that mortal hail from the clouds. Yet the oarsmen stuck to their job in the open craft.

Suddenly one sailor uttered a startled cry.

"What's the matter?" enquired his friend.

"Oh, it's nothing", he winced. "Keep going."

Then his friend looked again and watched the sailor with a sheath-knife digging a bullet out of a wounded leg.

Some of the bigger transports escaped annihilation not once but every trip, and in these modern days of oil-fuel plus overhead explosives there are risks which surpass conditions normal to the last war. One popular Scottish pleasure steamer performed especially good work, for her ample deck room made her ideal. One day they had crowded no fewer than 2500 troops aboard, and she was making fine progress from Dunkirk when the Nazi air squadrons determined to wipe her off the sea. Altogether five separate raids succeeded each other, yet only in the last did a bomb fall so near as to burst an oil pump.

CHAPTER XX — JOURNEY'S END

"THEY might have been waiting for a theatre to I open," was the impression conveyed by that disciplined line of soldiers waiting their turn to be taken aboard.

But when, that last night, the moon rose over the whole chaotic scene of destruction, Dunkirk might have been the Devil's playground. Battered ambulances scattered over the beach half covered by the tide, masts and funnels projecting from the water at drunken angles, naked horses galloping wildly over the sands indulging an artificial liberty; and all the while gunfire rumbling in the distance, bangs and flashes close to, the moaning whine of descending missiles; fights in the air, slaughter on land and sea.

Yet only one thing seemed to worry these valorous lads.

"What do they think of us at home? Does England say we've let the country down?" An officer in charge of a transporting craft told me this was the reaction after days of marching: weary footsloggers seemed to have forgotten all their other anxieties.

But never did a returning army have a more sympathetic welcome.

Of the small craft which took part in the withdrawal some never came back and had to be abandoned on the sands. One night there left an English port three tugs towing small boats. The first got safely to Dunkirk, the second lost her way and had to go back, but in the darkness the third was rammed by another vessel and sank. Nothing more has been heard either of the tug or her boats.

It was tricky work for seafarers by night standing in towards the beach on a falling tide. Some vessels got aground and could not be hauled afloat for hours, being bombed mercilessly in the meantime. Some, whilst steaming between the piers, would get their propeller fouled by the warps cast off from ships departing hurriedly, or the blades would be chipped off by a maze of wreckage. But the worst job was when a dinghy had to linger among breaking waves till one of the oarsmen landed, searched the black night for hiding soldiers, and began the boatloading with difficulty.

No wonder that, crowded to the gunwales, these dinghies and wherries would broach-to, fill up with sea, compelling everybody to leap overboard and begin again. I know of at least one case where the arrival of a soldier on board a motorboat brought so much dripping water that it stopped the engine.

Out of that hurly-burly our sailors, deafened by gunfire, their throats hoarse with shouting and the Dunkirk smoke, hauled into their shell-splintered craft unshaven men who might yet never see England. Private Allan of Blackburn swam most of two miles before reaching a boat and being picked up. His journey across the English Channel was accomplished safely, he travelled north to his home ... and found his mother had collapsed after receiving an official telegram that her son was missing.

Never was a crew nearer death than when a motorship coming from Dunkirk became the target for a Nazi airman. The warplane hovered, let go a missile which penetrated three decks and the transport's side. Yet not one casualty occurred, and the ship proceeded on her way. For the bomb was of the delayed-action type and did not explode till it fell harmlessly into the sea, by which time the vessel had got nicely ahead.

Had it been the season of winter, or of equinoctial gales, Dunkirk would have been not a miracle but a disaster. Beach work would have been impossible, small units could not have done their job, and the Germans must have reached the city all too soon for the rescuers.

It is true that a party of British soldiers with an officer discovered a small boat and set off for England. The officer knew enough to hoist and trim the sails, so the little band were able to travel fifteen miles and might have continued even further, but a vessel sighted them and gave the boat a tow for the remaining distance.

Seven more privates and one officer purloined a motor-boat, and got home without escort. Fine weather happened to make this venturing successful. The English Channel is rarely in the same mood for two successive days, and those motor-cruiser yachts overloaded with troops below, gear piled on cabin-top, were so crank that a beam wave almost sufficed to cause a capsize. Here is an instance.

Many readers will recollect when the White Star "Titanic" on her maiden voyage hit an iceberg and went down with a vast death roll. Among her survivors was an officer who lived to serve afloat during the war of 1914- 1918. Commander C. H. Lightoller, R.N.R., afterwards took to yachting, and just before the second war was cruising in his 58-footer "Sundowner" through Belgium and the Albert Canal that later became a pivot of history.

When the Dunkirk summons sounded in May 1940, the "Sundowner" was hastily fitted out, the Commander with his son and a Sea Scout took this motor-cruiser across, entered between the jetties and lay alongside a destroyer. Whilst the latter shelled the enemy, no fewer than 150 warriors — about four times more than permissible in peace time — were stowed away like potatoes.

They lay flat on the cabin floor, packed themselves tight round the diesel engine, some overflowed into the bath. When the "Sundowner" got out to sea, she felt like a saucer poised on a peak: one push, and over she would go. Exciting moments in mid-Channel when the double wash from British and French destroyers assailed her, but those fast ex-Dover-Calais steamers were almost as bad. The only thing was to stop engines, meet the waves bows-on, never mind the wetting or the groans of seasick soldiers.

The final scene in the Dunkirk drama ended at 7 a.m. of Tuesday, June 4, when the French Admiral Abrial departed. Throughout that night of terror, as the rearguard gradually withdrew through town to piers, holding off the enemy by house-to-house fighting till the very last, there were some desperate moments.

A British minesweeper was due to embark several hundred troops from the pier, but the tide being low this vessel could not get alongside. She touched the ground, and though engines were going full astern, stirring up the mud, she would not budge.

Terribly anxious climax! In twenty minutes the block-ships were to be sunk, and Dunkirk harbour corked up. Bombs exploded, Heinkels droned.

Then the harassed captain sighted one of our motor life-boats.

"Could you get a line on to the stern, and give us a pluck off?"

Disregarding all else, the life-boat dashed into this fiery comer, manoeuvred smartly, made fast the rope, and without snapping a hair of it worked up to full power. The strain was pretty heavy, the minesweeper still reluctant to shift.

Then, just as it seemed too late, she yielded and was hauled out into deeper water.

But hear the story of a French Infantry lieutenant who with nineteen of his men reached the seafront to discover the last transport gone, and the last destroyer departed. Germans pouring into the outskirts. Capture imminent.

The Frenchmen glanced round, searched the sands, found a small boat, bundled in, shoved off. Being completely ignorant of nautical matters, they were nonplussed by wind and tide. Presently the boat was swept alongside the wreck of what had once been a passenger steamer lying some four miles from the shore.

Not by any means a big ship, but at least her upper-works were well above high-tide. So the twenty unfortunates climbed aboard and then started to endure one of the most pathetic episodes of maritime suffering.

So near to land, yet so far from safety!

Deprived of food and water, they began to wonder whether their fate as prisoners would not have been better than starvation.

Nights became chilly, so they set fire to their boat in order to obtain warmth and in the hope of attracting rescuers.

No luck!

One party, resolved to fend for themselves, built a raft, started off, waved farewell. They were never seen again.

More than a week passed, Dunkirk's upheaval had faded into history, they could see the flames and smoke dying down, they knew that the Germans would be revelling among the booty. But never a ship now came in this direction.

Seven Frenchmen meanwhile perished — some by exposure, some by lack of food, but others through that tragic old error of drinking seawater.

Early on the evening of Wednesday, June 12, a British aeroplane flew over the area, came low, sighted nine semi-living survivors, and flashed the news across to a certain place on the English coast. Then things began to happen.

Picture a fast motor craft receiving urgent orders fifteen minutes later, engines being 'revved' up, moorings slipped, and the vessel speeding up at umpteen knots over the intervening North Sea. A race against destiny and oncoming darkness.

At the end of several hours as the time for dusk grew near, this isolated fragment of upperworks had yet to be located. Pretty hopeless to look for it in the dark among the Flemish shoals, and within range of the enemy's shore guns.

Moreover a nasty, treacherous sea soon rouses itself off Dunkirk without warning. The motor unit purred forward at pace. Out of the murk wheeled a couple of eagle-eyed British 'planes. They swooped lower still, led the way towards the half-sunken wreck, and just before the light began to fail, two lots of men mutually gazed over the white-crested expanse. A mere vague dot the upperworks stood out. A tiny speck, barely visible, seemed the rescuers.

As the latter approached and Frenchmen could be seen waving frantically, it became painfully obvious that to launch a dinghy in that boisterous sea would be hopeless: yet to take the motor craft alongside a steel hull would invite being smashed to bits.

Just then a large conflagration burst forth afresh on the land, accompanied by the roar of heavy gunfire. Had the Germans through their binoculars seen this mission of help?

No matter! The job had to be done. With extremely able skill the rescuing craft went up to the wreck, one by one the French officer, his eight men, their rifles and personal baggage with which they had set out — yes, and ludicrous to relate, their saxophone too — were all taken off, yet scarcely less wonderfully the motor vessel received no damage.

Then it was 'Homewards. Fast as you can make it!'

Through the gathering North Sea blackness, swishing spray from either side the bows, the rhythmical revolutions humming merrily as mileage was consumed. Long before the marine Good Samaritan got near the English coast deep night had cloaked everything. The sweet smell of land warned them it was time to slow down. Nearer approach would invite trouble from the vigilant shore defences. So the vessel let go anchor and decided to wait for dawn.

It is proof of our patrols' watchfulness that a trawler, which now came across her, was at first by no means satisfied. She needed a lot of convincing ere suspicion disappeared.

But with the coming of day the final difficulty vanished, the Frenchmen were landed where doctors and ambulances were ready to complete the rescue. Those nine days, marooned off their mother land would never be forgotten.

It is peril which brings forth personal pluck, and Dunkirk was full of both. One of the hotels was being used as a hospital when the time came for evacuation. Nearly four hundred and fifty men unable to walk. If only they could be sent across to England.

Hurriedly they were distributed among forty-three ambulances and sent towards the jetty. What a hope! German 'planes had no respect for that sort of thing, thus eleven ambulances never got there, being bombed and left flaming on the road: yet about three hundred wounded were tenderly propped up on the jetty near the lighthouse, seeking some shade from the blazing sun, but night finally enabled them to be taken off aboard the trawler "King George". They were still wearing pyjamas when they landed.

But another hundred and fifty wounded still waited on the beach in charge of the President of the French Army Nurses, Madame Casimir-Perier, widow of the grandson of the famous statesman. Her eyes looked eagerly towards a British destroyer anchored in the roadstead. But how could contact be made?

Willing to sacrifice her own life for others, she plunged into the sea, contended against the sluicing tide for three-quarters of an hour, and reached the destroyer, where they hauled her up still dripping with water and oil. The Captain came along, listened to the lady's plea, and presently the 150 were fetched alongside.

But it was a different British man-of-war which received fifteen hospital nurses weary and wet through, who now had the surprise of their lives. Sent down below to the limited cabin accommodation so willingly yielded, they were grateful for the warmth of blankets. Then, some hours later, as the ship was steaming into an English port they found their uniforms already cleaned, ironed, dried, ready to put on again.

You can't beat the Navy — even for hospitality!

Yet meanwhile Dunkirk beach was full of tragedy and pathos till the end. One of the bravest episodes centred round a gallant padre, the Rev. T. M. Layng, who already had won the Military Cross. Although the division to which he was attached had sailed away home, this chaplain remained behind looking after the wounded, burying the dead, whilst murderous bombs did their best to interrupt. At last he did reach England, and was justly awarded a bar to his M.C.

So the great drama of Dunkirk came to an end, 335,000 men were snatched from under the enemy's gaze. We cannot deny that German organisation was excellent, his callousness and brutality unparalleled, the momentum of his mechanised onslaughts amazing, his espionage and treachery diabolical.

But history will always associate Dunkirk with the miracle that was worked through our heroes by land, and air, and sea.

CHAPTER XXI — THE RAILWAYS HELP

ALL this effort by ships and men would have profited but little had not other departments of national activity collaborated to bring the tired, grimy, and mostly unshorn soldiers back to their British bases.

On Sunday, May 26, the Southern Railway at Dover was instructed to be ready for dealing with a large daily number of troops, who must pass through the port. Probably sixty trains would be needed in each twenty-four hours, and the men would arrive at all times.

Actually beginning from that memorable Monday the railway managed between May 27 and noon of Tuesday, June 4, to send no fewer than 35,000 soldiers from this harbour alone. The peak was reached on Friday, May 31, when 67 trains were despatched, though on another occasion as many as 7 ambulance trains were included. Obviously the ordinary passenger and freight trains had to be cut out of the railway schedule, but these landsmen were splendid fellows, tending their utmost aid in the great endeavour, working uncomplainingly for 24-hour stretches at a time.

One never knew at what hour to expect the arrival of some vessel dumping her fatigued human cargoes. For instance, the North Scottish pleasure steamer "Loch Garry" carried 2500 troops on one journey from Dunkirk. In the last five air attacks a bomb had dropped only a few yards away, an oil pump had burst and threatened to spray the fires with burning fluid. Disaster was avoided by the 37-years old fireman Martin Higgins of Stockport. She came into port with anxious soldiers longing only for safe transport further inland.

Such trains in the meanwhile had to fill up with four or five tons of coal and 4000 gallons of water, yet every half hour there would be one departing from Dover and it was possible to have similar arrangements at other ports. Ashore, the local people of their kindness brought forth refreshments to these transients; such organisations as the Church Army, the Salvation Army, the Y.M.C.A. with their mobile canteens flocked to see that the men who had fought should not perish of hunger by the English railside.

Several thousands of Frenchmen arriving with their rearguard were surprised to find in England no food shortage. They at first declined the proffered sandwiches till reassured. Neither soldiers, sailors, nor railway men had time in those strenuous days, still less the opportunity, for meals and rest. Ships came full of the living and the wounded, packed like boxed fish. How different was reality from theory, for at one time it looked as if we should be lucky to rescue 25,000. Who could have expected that more than thirteen times that number should cross the Channel?

And the stories these men brought with them were barely credible; how that a small group of our naval men had obtained barely one hour's sleep in twenty-four and were always short of food and water, the town of Dunkirk's water-supply having broken down during one of its earliest air-raids. Practically for six days the destroyer personnel off the French coast was at action stations, one such vessel making seven trips across, and usually she came back with 900 men as her guests.

Many of the London Fire Brigade and the Auxiliary men volunteered for this service and were disappointed that only the "Massey Shaw" of its firefloats was accepted. She measured 73 ft. long, 13½ ft. beam, with 3 ft. 9 in. draught, manned by a crew of eighteen. She was thus eminently suitable for the shallow waters, made three crossings and brought back 646 people: yet it is a fact that one night she spread consternation among some of our smaller craft in the roadstead. That object, familiar to firemen as the "monitor" for directing water on to conflagrations, looked to ordinary sailors so very like a gun that the appearance of it coming along through the darkness was at first worrying. Someone imagined the enemy had devised a new sort of power boat!

No braver epic of the sea in all its services has ever been attempted than the Dunkirk story: it was so universal that it affected everybody; the terrible grandeur left no one untouched, its majestic drama inspired by liberty will be related through all the ages. We are still living too near events to appreciate the supreme valour in one of the most glorious things ever attempted by mankind.

But we shall fail to understand why it was possible, why these light craft achieved the miracle, unless always the Royal Navy with its silent impressiveness somewhere up the North Sea was covering, and therefore supporting our advance forces, by day and night.

Had it not been for the nullifying influence of Sir Charles Forbes' battleships, cruisers and the like, we should certainly have had such of Hitler's surface ships as he could send to dominate those routes towards Dunkirk. Never was better illustrated the value of sea-power than the fact that these British coasters, paddlers, tugs, barges, and hundreds of others could go backwards and forwards over the English Channel in spite of aerial bombs and the guns erected on shore.

It was difficult and unfortunate that the narrow entrance of Dunkirk and a long stretch of sands were all that allowed for embarkation, yet those were at least better than the bare cliffs and beaches of Gallipoli. The real trouble was that essential haste, and the lack of such facilities as cranes, made it impossible to withdraw such heavy stores as tanks and our big guns.

Future historians will show that we had all the bad luck save once; that until breaking through the French Army near Sedan, and the overrunning of Holland, we were if in a tight corner at least fighting hard. Until the defection of the Belgian King the retreat of the Anglo-French forces was just a slow, almost leisurely, retreat in which the Allies counter-attacked. The enemy was unable to burst through the pocket of a narrow corridor until Leopold had opened up for the Germans a road leading to Dunkirk.

The duty, the discipline, the self-sacrificing valour of all seafarers on behalf of the Army is something that we can never forget because it transcends any episode which has ever occurred in our long island story; but it was so characteristic of the united national effort that comprised railwaymen and industrial workers. Typically German was the enemy's resolve to win by the ruthless employment of massed men, the accumulation of stores; by his mechanisation and treachery. Typically British was our stubborn refusal to acknowledge defeat in the gravest of hours.

That men after fighting and swimming canals should live several days on biscuits in hollowed-out dunes, then swim, row, or wade out to waiting boats under continuous fire, is at least an example of endurance, but it had only been practicable whilst defensive positions were being held and the perimeter being gradually narrowed. The entrenched camp of Dunkirk was protected by a line of defence known as the Corunna Line; but the flooding of the Yser valley and further inundation stretching from Gravelines to the southwest decidedly helped in checking the enemy's advance.

If this was the first time that an army on passage over the sea was assaulted by air power, theoretically not one of our transports should have crossed, let alone voyaging many times. Sea power was thus to have the last say.

We shall never have the full story of the many adventures, though in the previous pages some attempt has been made to record the most possible while still men are existing — men who took such a prominent part in the biggest event of their lives. There is a wealth of tragedy belonging to those who were the last to get away from burning Dunkirk in whatever boats could be found; the stories of men and officers in turns rowing over the tides, of some forlorn figure sitting in the stern to steer by his pocket compass.

One boat full of sailors and soldiers was capsized and then righted. She reached a lightship, secured to the stern, whilst her men were hauled aboard to lie down and sleep. It was such a free-for-all adventure as not even the Elizabethans would have dared to leave their homes for in search of the more than ordinary. Every kind of unusual happening was ready for everybody, and the most assorted kind of volunteers was forthcoming: managing directors and clerks going straight from city offices, labourers and artisans, technical experts and amateur yachtsmen; all placed their lives and hopes on the national behalf. One old man from Deal came to Dunkirk in a boat named the "Dumpling". She was so aged that when this craft was built the battle of Waterloo had not yet been won. And it was bad luck that after a septuagenarian naval pensioner with one boy for three days and nights made trips in a motorboat to a shell-spattered beach, this craft should be sunk on the seventh time by the wash from two high-powered British destroyers.

England expected those days that every man would do his duty: and he did it. To the home-coming soldiers the white cliffs of Dover looked more than the gateway of home. The inspiring sight of H.M. ships racing at top speed, anxious not to waste a moment, was unforgettable, and commanding officers have told me how these soldiers at the end of the trip tried in their own way from the gangway to utter their thanks for the Navy's care. But there were many of the helpers who as employees of the railways were able to waft these men inland. We must not omit those overworked shore staffs, the crane drivers, porters who helped wounded men ashore, the stretcher-bearers of more serious cases, the locomotive drivers, those others who coaled and fuelled vessels that they might do a record 'turn round'. It was evidence of our united efforts that provisions were suddenly supplied from nowhere, that shipwrecked men bereft of everything were supplied with clothes.

No wonder, then, when Dunkirk was over that the Board of Admiralty on June 4 sent a general signal congratulating all concerned for a most brilliant evacuation. This department referred to "the physical strain imposed by long hours of arduous work in narrow waters over many days". Nor did the Admiralty exaggerate in adding that "the ready willingness with which seamen from every walk of life came forward to assist their brother seamen of the Royal Navy will not readily be forgotten."

To ninety-one of the Merchant ships — 57 passenger and store vessels, plus the 34 tugs — was sent the following letter by Mr Ronald Cross, Minister of Shipping, in gratitude and admiration:

"This operation, in which the Merchant Navy joined as partner of the fighting services, was carried to a successful conclusion in the face of difficulties never before experienced in war. I am proud to pay tribute to your share and that of your ship's company in a great and human adventure destined to occupy a place of honour in the pages of history."

CHAPTER XXII — THE SECRET OF SUCCESS

INCLUDED in the 222 British Royal Naval vessels were several flotillas of destroyers, but also were such units as minesweepers, minelayers, motor torpedo boats, and others. The 665 other British but mercantile craft plus numbers of French vessels comprised the whole force. A remnant of the Belgian Army came with that evacuation because, after the order had been issued to cease fire against the enemy, some Belgian officers refused to hand over their revolvers but made for the coast. The Dunkirk embarkation being protected by our tanks, Field Artillery, massed Bren and Bofors guns, could not however control either the harbour's width or its depth.

The entrance channel of 443 feet between the two pile jetties provided less than the required and expected 15 feet at Low Water. Those basins within, the docks and locks, the yards for repairing and building of ships, were quite useless, and the 3-knots tide which about High Water Springs rushes past the mouth were features new to many commanding officers. Although some groped with their craft in the darkness on the port hand after getting inside, there ensued much confusion, and it was really the jetties which mattered, but fortunately the tide (though bad enough for the boats which had to be rowed from the beaches) did not during those days quite attain its greatest velocity.

Normally, too, the approach to Dunkirk is via the Dyck lightship in the West Pass, but the several more direct routes by cutting across the Flemish banks were made use of at this time by various vessels. As the gull flies, the distance from Ramsgate to Dunkirk is roughly forty miles in a southeast direction, but most of the deeper draft ships were compelled to go further round so as to avoid the shoals.

The surprising feature is not that an occasional vessel got ashore but that the losses from all causes were so few, although aeroplanes and land batteries did their very worst. In addition to the six destroyers, "Grafton", "Grenade", "Wakeful", "Basilisk", "Keith" and "Havant", the Royal Navy lost the following minor units: "Skipjack", "Mosquito", "Grive" (better known as the Steam Yacht "Narcissus"), "Brighton Belle",

"Gracie Fields", "Waverley", "Medway Queen", "Brighton Queen", "Crested Eagle", the two armed boarding vessels "King Orry" and "Mona's Isle", the dan-laying vessel "Comfort", the tug "St. Fagan", and also the eight trawlers "Polly Johnston", "Thomas Bartlett", "Thuringia", "Calvi", "Stella Dorado", "Argyllshire", "Blackburn Rovers" and "Westella", together with the three drifters "Girl Pamela", "Paxton", and "Rob Roy". Total twenty-four. This, of course, does not include all those other purely mercantile ships lost during their temporary association with the Navy at this period. Of these due notice has been taken in other chapters, as for instance the loss of that fine cross-Channel steamer "Paris" whilst serving as a hospital ship and clearly marked as such with the Red Cross.

There were many side issues which belong to our subject that are not part of the main theme, yet by throwing gleams of sidelight they illuminate this vast picture. One of the Dutch craft taken over by the Navy arrived off Dunkirk minus charts. These had been blown away when a bomb struck her whilst outward bound. But whosoever might be the adventurer — whether naval officer or rating, experienced master mariner or yachtsman — the most vivid memory is not that of many vessels racing across the sea but of Dunkirk's sky dotted like flies with German bombers and of the immense fires burning along the coast, the cranes and derricks of the quayside silhouetted against the flames.

Neither pleasant nor easy in the darkness was the work of inshore boats. Lashed fore and aft alongside a ship's motor launch, some of them eventually were anchored and then backed down stern-first towards the beach so as to cheat the ebbing tide and come off more easily with a complement of soldiers. It might be awkward, after removing boots and socks, to step out of the boat and go looking for troops sheltering among the dunes; it was still more tiresome on the return journey after the crowded boat broached-to, filled, had to be emptied and the whole thing begun afresh. It needs no further emphasis that when for two days a northerly wind blew briskly against those shores it demanded all human effort to perform this boat-work without disaster, and only for one afternoon did ground mist curtail enemy activity.

But there must have been singularly stupid German aviators in the sky, for they insisted on magnifying every destroyer into a battleship and every trawler into a cruiser. The possibility of battleships and cruisers being found so near to the beach is a delightful fantasy incomprehensible to any seafaring man. It has been reckoned that 300 French warships and merchantmen plus 200 of their smaller craft assisted, and they lost the destroyers "Chacal", "L'Adroit", "Bourrasque", "Foudroyant", "Ouragan" and "Sirocco", but it should be pointed out that both "L'Adroit" and their supply ship "Niger" had been sunk just before these evacuation attempts were made. It was more than so much tonnage thrown away when that fine 1300-tons "Sirocco" went down, for on various occasions she had distinguished herself by sinking three U-boats.

The Germans claimed at 5-15 p.m. of June 5 to have captured Dunkirk with many prisoners and "an incalculable quantity of war material", but they found after our departure a city of the dead, a port where the grass had been burned brown, the streets all crater holes, and on either hand were the graves of men who had just missed their transference to England. More than 80 divisions were used by the enemy in his Battle of the Ports, 10 being armoured divisions and 5 comprising motorised infantry. Between May 10 and June 6 it is believed that the Germans lost more than 400,000 of their 2,500,000 troops.

How some of our own soldiers managed to evade fate and gain their ships makes one more than ever wonder at human endurance and ingenuity. In one part of Dunkirk were 81 of our men sheltering in a big cellar during a heavy air raid when five bombs wrecked the place and set the building on fire, so that they were badly trapped and could not get away. The cellar was growing hotter and hotter, the soldiers getting weaker and weaker, and no air filtering through.

What was to be done?

They all made as much possible noise with their dixies and sang with loud voices, and at length a strange voice from somewhere outside bellowed back.

"Where are you?"

And these men sought to indicate their position.

Through two hours this anonymous helper tried breaking through the awful debris, and he succeeded in passing a piece of lead-piping.

"Look out! I'm pouring some drink down to keep you going till I can get better tools."

Meanwhile the heavy thud of bombs continued to fall.

Then after an interval the helper returned with a lorry, a chisel and a hammer.

"Hold on tight!", he shouted. "And hope for the best."

Another bang, a shower of bricks and dust. Once more the voice.

"Believe I've done it."

He had made a hole big enough to crawl through, but so exhausted were those imprisoned that he had to help them out. With his lorry he had collected wines, cakes, sweets, and tinned foods. They started to thank him, but he wouldn't listen.

"That's my hobby", answered the other, "risking my life gives me quite a kick."

He then surprised his astonished spectators still more by fetching a brown bag from the lorry, and doing conjuring tricks for their benefit.

Now this good friend happened to be a Lance-bombardier in the early forties who, in the First German War had served as a despatch-rider, but in times of peace became a famous T.T. rider, a sensational performer on the stage in the "Wall of Death", and also a public-house proprietor. He later explained, in freeing this Dunkirk cellar from the certain death which seemed to hold the 81 captives, that he placed French hand-grenades into the wall, pulled out the pins, then dived for shelter beneath his lorry.

But so excited was he after the explosion that he jumped to his feet, banged his head against the chassis and was rendered temporarily unconscious. A great fellow, this ex-actor followed up the conjuring incident by jumping into the lorry and, racing round the town, picked up a score of wounded men. These he carried one by one on to the vehicle, and deposited at the First Aid station.

Finally wearied out with his adventures, he drove four miles beyond Dunkirk, camouflaged the lorry with straw and slept a while. Meeting some French soldiers, he was given some coffee and drove back to Dunkirk beach looking for more trouble but furnished with food and rum for others. Down flew the aeroplanes, bang went the bombs. He took refuge in a ditch. When he emerged, there was no longer any lorry excepting a few bits and pieces. So, having spent from Monday to Saturday helping the wounded as best he could, he set off for England with other evacuees aboard a steamer, carrying as a souvenir one scrap of that wooden lorry which had played so important a chapter in his and other lives.

What especially infuriated the British soldiers was to witness the aeroplanes diving to slay Red Cross nurses who for days were defying bombs, bullets, and shells whilst tending casualties on the beach. Yet most heroically these women refused to be taken away till the last of the B.E.F. wounded had been removed to safety. It was self-sacrifice which thus caused death to nurses, though some were lucky only to receive wounds. Without sleep they had toiled among the awful dunes for days amid the whistling missiles, dragging heavy men to improvised shelter, fetching them food and water, helping others down to the rescuing boats, even wading themselves into the sea.

That same indomitable spirit pervaded the hospital ship "Paris" when she was bombed and the boats had to be loaded, but even then the aircraft swooped till they left nurses with bleeding faces or — in one case — a shattered arm. Although boats were holed and one nurse was blown high in the air, and the ship had to be abandoned, not one of these gallant women was killed, though Peter Puddock, a 17-year deck boy, was killed by the bullets. Of course the destruction of the oil-tanks which formerly held 2,000,000 gallons of petrol made an easy mark for the distant German 5.9-inch guns, or they could aim at the jetties, or they would foolishly concentrate at the wrecks.

Two of the last British soldiers to leave were Corporal G. Huntington (of Nottingham) and Private J. Cowlam (of Hull), both belonging to the East Yorkshire Regiment. They had many an experience difficult to be narrated in cold print. As a preliminary, they were amongst those who swam canals to gain the Dunkirk sands, where they existed for three days and then scrambled aboard a launch that was leaving the beach.

This launch was blown from under them, their equipment and pouches blasted off their backs, yet they again swam, and this time towards an old barge, where they sat till a French boat picked them up on June 4.

Astounding, too, was the escape of two girls. Elaine Madden, aged 17, was daughter of a British gardener employed by the War Graves Commission at Poperinghe. The father had joined the British Army but she had remained behind tending the British graves of the First War. With her was associated Simone Duponselle, two or three years older, a sister of Elaine's mother who kept the Palace Hotel in the Rue d'Ypres, Poperinghe.

Trudging their way from Poperinghe bound towards Dunkirk, these two women were found by a British sergeant and two privates of the Dorsetshire Regiment who gave them a lift in their car. After having been bombed for five days in Poperinghe and witnessing the streets on fire, the two young persons had left their town on May 28 at 5-30 a.m. with blankets across their shoulders and a few belongings in their bags.

After five miles' progress they had to take cover in a barn as German tanks were occupying the fields on either side of the road, and it was at the end of another five miles that the British soldiers were met with. Everything was going moderately well till at the end of twenty miles they all were compelled to get out as German 'planes were coming over destroying all bridges; but the three khaki men helped them across country, giving them even their coats and steel helmets, and at last the girls reached the main road to Dunkirk where they obtained another lift in an Army lorry towards the quayside.

With the sympathy and kindness for the distressed, British 'Tommies' allowed the pair of escapers to mingle with the crowd which foot by foot was moving along the jetty towards the waiting steamer. 'Tin' hat plus tunic concealed in the crowd a great deal, but the crisis came when the iron ladder had to be climbed down. Simone went first.

Then an observant man, remembering Fifth Columnists, immediately recognised the feminine legs.

"Hullo! There's a woman coming aboard."

"No! No!" denied the impersonator, but it was hardly convincing.

As a result the brace of damsels were brought before the Captain, explanations followed, and eventually they were landed safely in England.

Several days later arrived 68 members of the French infantry belonging to the 85th Regiment. They were part of the Dunkirk garrison who so nobly fought under Vice-Admiral Jean Abrial till the very end, and made the withdrawal of others possible. They contended in fact till the early hours of Tuesday, June 4, when, their ammunition being exhausted and German tanks as advance parties closing into the streets, these Frenchmen with grenades, or rifle-butts, or their bayonets, made the best of things while some went to see what boats could be found for their retreat.

At the jetty the best were two which had been damaged by bombs. Some decided to trust themselves to a rowing boat in spite of machine-gun fire and till well past daylight they rowed about not knowing in what direction. Then they sighted a vessel with other soldiers of the regiment and threw in their lot with them, and Tuesday was an anxious day in the tideway drifting along the English Channel when a defunct motor refused to help. But one of the R.N.L.I. life-boats off the English coast put out early on June 5 and brought these soldiers into safety.

And other small craft after the final Dunkirk evacuation were spasmodically also arriving off our shores for a day or two following immediately after their final battling. In some cases the men had neither eaten nor drank during 40 hours, and they were considerably surprised that in England was plenty of food to satisfy the most ravenous.

Looking back on those remarkable days, we can congratulate ourselves that the losses of ships and men were so small considering the gamble was so great. It was imperative that — whatever the cost — those soldiers entrusted to the different branches of the Sea Service should be landed on English soil. The reader will have noted that in spite of all the enemy's efforts not many vessels had been sacrificed; but of the Merchant Navy were 121 killed and 79 wounded, whilst among the civilian volunteers were 4 killed and 2 wounded.

Survivors, however, will remember Dunkirk's realistic pictures as long as life lasts. They will never forget the enemy's callousness and brutality any more than the burning fires on land and the pyramids of water leaping from the shallows as bombs virulently lifted and dropped the ships. They will always remember destroyers shaking with the recoil of guns, those bright yellow flashes … the crash … and the cloud of smoke that once was a fine ship. The sound of gunfire will always rumble in their ears, the taste of smoke will not be disassociated from hoarse sore throats. They will never watch a man wading into the sea without calling to mind those who trod the awful sands neck deep.

The memory cannot banish boats laden to the gunwale, nor the dog-fights going on above, nor those thumb-nail fleeting impressions of sailors in duffle coats and sea-boots resisting all tendency to sleep. Rich man, poor man, longshoreman, fisherman, yachtsman — they were all the same on one common denominator.

To those who came back sensitive to sights and smells one of the saddest memories is of visible wreckage, funnels and upper works riddled with splinters, masts and White Ensign still there; the moon peeping out behind a cloud at the long lines of men awaiting their turn to be taken off homewards. Soldiers burly and brown, but very tired, stand back for the stretcher cases lowered aboard ship between the bursts of typical German rhythmical explosions at the mole, destroyers firing guns as they entered churning the water, the click of scaling ladders placed from ship to jetty.

When the War Office announced on June 4 that the evacuation of Allied Forces had been successfully completed, and called it "one of the most difficult operations of war undertaken", when also the Admiralty claimed this to have been "the most extensive and difficult combined operation in Naval history", no one could allege that in these two statements there had been the slightest overemphasis.

Aloft the Coastal Command's aircraft were co-operating with those of the Navy, maintaining ceaseless patrols to assist the B.E.F.'s departure, though we could have done with many more in the sky. Thanks to flooding, and thanks likewise to the relentless daring of our Royal Air Force, the interference with our withdrawal was not greater than it actually might have been, and the casualties alike on beaches and inland were amazingly few. The main onslaught of German bombers directed against our shipping was an expression of the fear that after all our merchantmen were defeating the worst blasts that ever came out of sky or shore.

Whatever else may have been proved, the value of existing organisations and of those newly devised demonstrated outstandingly that there is always some dormant power in the British national character ready to be summoned for big occasions. It does not admit of its own existence, yet nothing is allowed to kill it and time cannot modify that ability in its successive generations. As it volunteered for the Boer War, so it rose for the First and Second Wars against Germany; but in particular this Dunkirk affair was exactly suited to our innate love of attempting the most difficult and dangerous things with a coolness and determination which no one else better than ourselves can understand.

And we are thankful that this is so.

[1] See Chapter III.

CHAPTER VII — THE TASK FOR SEAFARERS

[2] Much used in dredging the Thames channels.

CHAPTER XI — THE LIFE SAVERS

[3] See Chapter I.

CHAPTER XIII — THE SHIPS CARRY ON

[4] Compare the latter's report in Chapter XV.

[5] See Chapter XII.

CHAPTER XV — HELL'S DELIGHT

[6] See Chapter XI.

CHAPTER II — TOWARDS DUNKIRK
CHAPTER XVI — THE TUGS GO TO IT

[7] See Chapter IX.

Made in the USA
Middletown, DE
07 June 2017